COUNTRY
RAGAMUFFINS

COUNTRY RAGAMUFFINS

Reflections on a
Midwestern Farm Childhood

MAXINE BERGERSON WERNER

TWO HARBORS PRESS

Two Harbors Press
322 First Avenue N, 5th floor
Minneapolis, MN 55401
612.455.2293
www.TwoHarborsPress.com

ISBN-13: 978-1-62652-271-8
LCCN: 2013911987

Distributed by Itasca Books

Printed in the United States of America

"The land is the only thing in the world worth working for, worth fighting for, worth dying for, because it's the only thing that lasts."

~ Gerald O'Hara, *Gone With the Wind*

TABLE OF CONTENTS

INTRODUCTION..ix

PART ONE: FAMILY

Norwegian Buffoonery 1

Depot Agent...7

Eight Ragamuffins...13

Grandma Galena 23

PART TWO: HOME

The Home Place 33

A Symphony of Seasons..43

PART THREE: WORK

Barn chores..55

Don't Pop the Clutch 65

Cooking and Baking from Scratch...................................73

Garden Produce and a Blue Speckled Canner 83

Wringer Washer...91

Cleanliness Is Next to Godliness 95

Allowance 99

PART FOUR: PLAY

Put an Egg in Your Shoe and Beat It...............................105

Summer Evenings 115

Hunting and fishing..121

High Card Deals..127

Radio Flyer Sleds 133

Hardcover Friends 139

Part five: Family Folkways

Irish Relatives 147

Flour Sack Dresses 151

Cod Liver Oil 157

Part Six: Holidays

Fourth of July Picnic 163

Halloween 167

A Season of Joy and Peace 171

Christmas on the Farm 189

Part seven: Community

Visiting 201

Community Culture 209

Our Town 217

4-H Country Club 223

Rural School 229

Part Eight: Serious subjects

Religious Influences 243

Endless Talking 251

Epilogue 257

Part Nine: Appendix

From Grandma Galena's Recipe Box 265

INTRODUCTION

Every Family Tells a Story

This book is an introspective journey back to the time of my child-hood on a Minnesota farm during the 1950s and '60s. It is the story of a place and its people, who were shaped by the spirit and heritage of life in a Norwegian farming community. Change during the 1950s and '60s was pervasive and profound. A story not told is lost forever. My goal is to preserve the life experiences, attitudes, and values of my childhood before those memories grow dim and finally disappear. I hope to convey the character of a Midwestern rural community and of a typical farm family of the time.

Our grandmother, Galena Hilaria Hansel Bergerson (1898–1975), was a significant influence on our childhood. This is the story of a grandmother who passed along a deep appreciation of her Norwegian cultural heritage to the generations who followed.

Dad, Milton Orin Bergerson (1923–1983), and Mom, Madalen Jane Nagle Bergerson (1925–2010), grew to adulthood during two tumultuous and painful decades of war and depression. My father was born on the farm he would work and reside on for his entire life. He was raised with three brothers in a Norwegian-speaking community his grandparents had helped to settle. This is the story of my father, who transitioned from horsepower to tractor power and who never wavered in his love for the land and the independent life of a farmer.

My mother, raised in an Irish Catholic family and community in North Dakota, was disposed during World War II by the Great Northern Railway to be a depot agent in the Lutheran community of Dalton, Minnesota. Here she met and fell in love with my father. My parents married across religious boundaries of that time. As the sole Catholic in her new community, Mom reared eight children with resoluteness and determination; and with boundless energy and vitality, she worked relentlessly as a farm wife.

This is the story of eight siblings whose collective strength and work contributions played a vital part in family survival, during a time when Minnesota farm families relied heavily on children for a labor force. As sons and daughters, we contributed significantly by taking care of livestock, helping with field work, collecting eggs, cooking meals, washing clothes, and caring for our younger siblings. Raised during a generation that socialized and educated children to a gender-based division of labor, my father considered "man's work" inappropriate for girls. However, blessed with an abundance of girls, he had no choice but to have his daughters provide the workforce for barn chores, hauling hay, picking rock, grinding feed, and numerous other farm duties. We girls spent our time performing a wide range of domestic tasks as well as handling barn and field chores. Birth order, not gender, determined who did the "man's work."

Life on the farm was a tapestry of work and play. One of our parents' greatest strengths was their understanding of the benefits of play as well as work. Perhaps this was inherent for them because they enjoyed play themselves. During playtime hours, we roamed the farm, doing whatever our imaginations conceived. Living in the country, we became best friends with our siblings.

This is the story of the land of my childhood that remains in my heart. Country life cultivated in us a powerful bond with and deep appreciation for our natural world. A sense of place evolved as we experienced the serenity and rapture of the land during the four diverse seasons. The rewards of country living were momentous as we enjoyed unbridled explorations around rolling fields, pastures, and woodland.

Historically, this time and place provided the foundation for my happy childhood. I grew up during an era when the family farm and small-town living defined Minnesota rural life. Many of our experiences focused on kinship and connectedness with the local community. Friends and neighbors gave labor freely with the understanding that, eventually, the favor would be returned. Visiting with neighbors and relatives on Friday nights and Sunday afternoons were social engagements we anticipated each week.

School was a fundamental part of our lives and something we cherished. We attended a three-room country school for eight years; and for all eight years, I had the same four classmates.

I was part of the last generation that used an outhouse rather than indoor plumbing, took baths in a galvanized washtub, and slept in an unheated room upstairs. A kitchen wood stove and a dining room oil heater provided the heat for our house. We did have electricity; but we did not have a television, freezer, electric range, or electric dryer.

This is a story about things that were deeply meaningful to me: family, the blend of work and play, the beauty of the land, the sense of community, and the value of education. I can still see and hear a house filled with laughter, conversation, and debate. I can still feel the joy of celebrating holidays, seeing newborn babies coming home from the hospital, and feeling myself swaying high atop a wagonload of June hay on the way to the barn.

Writing this book was a labor of love. My brothers and sisters helped piece together the scattered recollections of years now long past. Each sibling has different memories shaped by birth order, but we all feel blessed with good family, friends and neighbors, and the natural, rural beauty we shared on the farm. Those of us who remember that era are a dying breed.

Even when I am old and gray, do not forsake me, O God, till I declare your power to the next generation, your might to all who are to come.
–Psalm 71:18 (NIV)

PART ONE

Family

Mom and Dad 1947

CHAPTER 1

Norwegian Buffoonery

The second of four boys, Dad was born on the farm in 1926. His parents, Palmer and Galena, were the grandchildren of Norwegian immigrants, and Norwegian was Dad's first language. At a time when many rural kids quit school after the eighth grade, Dad roomed in Fergus Falls for four years to finish high school (a distance too far to commute daily). Two sons continued to farm the land after Grandpa and Grandma retired to town; but with the modernization of equipment, two families could not make a living on this land. Dad, being the oldest son who wished to stay, received that opportunity.

Dad's passion for farming came from deep within his heart. Throughout his life, he plowed, planted, and harvested corn, oats, wheat, and alfalfa, and he cared for cattle and pigs. For Dad, there was no better existence than being a farmer. He loved the rural lifestyle, farming the land, and having a strong identity in a local community.

Initially, Dad used horses for fieldwork; they pulled machines such as drills, discs, harrows, cultivators, binders, and plows. However, by the late 1930s, tractors replaced his horses, and Dad witnessed a sharp rise in productivity per acre when he changed from horse-powered farming to tractor farming. Dad farmed during a time of rapid change in the American farming industry, and he embraced the changes, utilizing new methods of planting, fertilizing, cultivating, and harvesting. The *Farm Journal* and *Successful Farming* magazines became Dad's textbooks, and he read them with discernment and an open mind.

Reading and Smoking

My father's six-foot-five-inch distinguished stature, jet-black hair, and deep brown skin—sun-baked and leathered from his time on the tractor—gave him a Native American appearance. He whistled as he drove his blue pickup truck into town each morning, resting his arm out an open window and giving oncoming motorists his one-finger wave. He delivered cream and milk cans to the creamery; then continued on to his Uncle Roy's café to drink black coffee, tell jokes, and talk farm business with the locals. When one of us kids accompanied him, Dad bought us a Nesbitt's orange pop or a Hines root beer to sip while we spun on the chrome-legged stools with red vinyl seats. He never left the café without buying a bag of candy bars for his children at home.

In the evenings, Dad settled himself at the kitchen table with a cup of steaming coffee, his chambray shirt sleeves rolled up to his elbows, a bulging Salem cigarette pack in the pocket, and a cigarette in hand. Engrossed in a book, magazine, or newspaper, he was oblivious to "Your Cheating Heart" droning from the radio or any of the other commotion in the room.

When I was growing up, it seemed like most men smoked. I never saw a woman smoke. Every house I knew had ashtrays in every room. A fancy ashtray on a stand would adorn the living room, and there was always a glass ashtray on the kitchen table. My dad smoked three or four packs a day, in the house and out of the house. I must have been so used to the smoke that I thought nothing of it. I am not aware if Dad knew about the health risks of smoking, but I am sure he had not heard of the dangers of secondhand smoke.

Family First

Dad lived his life with decency and morality. He did not tell dirty jokes or swear in front of women or kids. We seldom saw him get angry. He gave to those in need without fanfare, lent neighbors a helping hand, and made a conscious choice to treat others with kindness. He performed his civic commitment by being a member of the school board and the township board. Dad taught us that happiness depends less upon circumstances than attitude. Mom and Dad placed family first and made extreme sacrifices for us kids. If anyone asked Dad what his greatest accomplishment in life was, he would answer, "My children."

Embracing Life with Humor

Dad, a charismatic, brilliant man, captured our imaginations and taught us to embrace life with humor. He used laughter to cheer us up and to make work fun. He encouraged us to laugh at ourselves and not to take ourselves too seriously.

Dad was excited about life and family, and he made his enthusiasm known to others through his quick wit and humor and by spinning tall tales. We enjoyed the silliness he showed by wiggling his ears, "pulling his thumb off," performing card tricks, and mysteriously extracting a quarter from his ear. His lighthearted spoofing convinced us kids to explore for gold and attempt to dig a hole to China. Dad's humor and enthusiasm were contagious. People from all areas of his life enjoyed listening to his jokes, his stories, and his hearty laugh.

Storytelling was Dad's art form, and we kids were not always sure what was make-believe and what was real. According to Dad, Norwegian elves with red caps were living in our barn. In exchange for a place to stay, they secretly helped Dad with the chores. Dad swore it was true.

Another of his tales concerned leprechauns. One summer morning, Dad appeared at the door with his usual mischievous grin on his face. "I'll be danged! I spotted two leprechauns standing by our lilac hedge."

"Oh, really?" Mom raised her eyebrows and glanced at us kids.

"I bet we're the only farm in Tumili Township with leprechauns," Dad said. "I heard they only visit a farmstead if an Irish person lives there."

"Really, Milton?" Mom said.

"Yep, and if we find their pot of gold, we will be rich." Dad poured himself a cup of coffee and sat at the table.

"Dad, what did they look like?" we asked.

"They were little men in green suits." Dad shut his eyes to think. "The one with a hole in his pants held a crock of gold while the other one carried a spade."

"Wow!" We struggled to distinguish reality from fantasy with Dad; but, as always, he swore it was true.

Dad smiled, "I know for a fact that if you capture one, he will direct you to their pot of gold."

When my siblings and I visited our playhouse that afternoon, we discovered that leprechauns had indeed visited and left us coins! For one week, we planned how to capture the leprechauns. We designed a perfect lookout, decided how to signal each other when we spied them, and tried to determine what we would say to the little men in green.

One day at the dinner table, my brother Daryl announced, "I talked to the leprechauns this morning."

We stared at Daryl. "What did you talk about?"

"We just talked," he said, piling food on his plate. "I can't remember what they said."

"I knew they would connect with one of you," Dad said with pride, winking at Daryl.

That night, leprechauns left several coins under Daryl's pillow. Over time, we other kids grew leery of looking for leprechauns. Dad and Daryl were the only ones who ever saw them.

He will turn the hearts of the parents to their children,
and the hearts of the children to their parents . . .
–Malachi 4:6 (NIV)

CHAPTER 2

Depot Agent

Mom was raised in an Irish Catholic family in rural Manvel, North Dakota, but World War II brought her across the border to Minnesota. When our country entered the war, the Great Northern Railway recruited many women, including Mom, to fill gaps left by male employees who joined the United States armed forces. Mom received training at a telegraph school, learned Morse code and telegraphy operations, and served three years as a depot agent in the North Dakota and Minnesota towns of Hillsboro, Niagara, Thompson, Dalton, Hallock, Harwood, and Rothsay.

As she was dispatched from town to town, breaking gender boundaries in her career, living alone as a single young woman, and making new friends, Mom's courage and independence escalated. She developed a fierce self-reliance and confidence as a woman in a "man's world." As a ticket agent, station operator, and railroad freight agent, Mom monitored communications for the dispatcher, copied Western Union telegrams in Morse code, handled freight that was delivered to the freight house, and sold tickets to the public. Gasping and holding her breath, she would hold out a stick in her outstretched arm to hand messages to engineers, who grabbed them as their train zoomed by. She observed tearful farewells of service members who departed by train. With tears she informed loved ones when a service member returned home by casket. Getting a telegram (many people did not have telephones) during the war was scary because so often they carried bad news.

World War II etched memories into Mom's mind that she could not erase. She shared stories with us about air-raid drills, blackouts, and salvage efforts. She talked about the ration books for sugar, shoes, gasoline, and other items in limited supply. Her two brothers made it safely through the war, but her brother-in-law did not. She sang "When the Lights Go On Again All Over the World" enough times that I still have the words etched in my mind:

"When the lights go on again all over the world
And the boys are home again all over the world"

A New Home

While Mom was serving as a depot agent in the Norwegian Lutheran community of Dalton, she met and fell in love with Dad. As a new bride, Mom left the life she had known and loved in her Irish Catholic community and moved to a new cultural environment, becoming the first Catholic in Dalton. This move took her 150 miles away from her hometown and family, so she kept in touch with her relatives through letters, and she looked forward to seeing them each summer.

Over the years, Mom started to resemble a Norwegian, but not a Lutheran. She held steadfast to her Catholic religion and raised us kids Catholic, though Dad never "turned." She was able to comfortably be the sole Catholic in a Lutheran community because Dad's Lutheran family and friends embraced and accepted her with unconditional love. Mom was never considered an outsider. She was Milton's wife and, as such, she was accepted as part of the web of his close-knit community.

A Firm but Loving Mother

Mom and Dad were equal partners in their marriage when it came to decision making. Mom, an independent and determined woman, bore eight healthy children in a sixteen-year timespan. A firm parent, she did not tolerate laziness, fighting, or sassing. She maintained order in her house by having us adhere to schedules and rules; and although she scolded and reproved us kids when we did wrong, she loved and protected us and wanted us to have a meaningful life. Practical, pragmatic, and not given to sentiment, Mom refused to revert to tact or charm to gain something she wanted. She spoke her mind and did not give in to self-indulgence.

The Rewards of Homemaking

For Mom, homemaking was a lifetime commitment and a dignified profession. She never felt ensnared by the hard life of a farm wife—in fact, she found many rewards in it. Shiny waxed floors, a weed-free garden, and well-behaved children gave her a sense of accomplishment. She appreciated the artistry in rows of canned peaches, the aroma of freshly baked bread, the ambiance of a room filled with a lilac bouquet, and Sunday dinners enjoyed by family in the dining room.

The long hours of labor Mom put in as a farm wife and mother of eight are quite daunting to me. Her only domestic help during her pregnancies or even in time of sickness was her daughters. The almost constant work—without benefit of modern conveniences and improvements—was labor intensive and largely a matter of brawn. We did not have a bathroom installed in the house until after her seventh child was born, and rather than relying on an automatic washer and dryer, Mom washed everything in a wringer washing machine and hung our wash on the line in both summer and winter.

Although she never showed signs of physical exhaustion, the strain of bearing eight children and carrying a heavy workload did take a toll on Mom's health. She wrapped her legs daily because of swollen, twisted, and painful varicose veins. Dad always tried to make her burden easier by asking us girls to help more around the house.

Leisure Interests

Rural life and eight children took up most of Mom's time and energy. She was the one who coordinated get-togethers, school activities, and family happenings. Although she cared little for social status, Mom always preferred socializing over a good rest. She took great pleasure in entertaining, playing cards, bowling, and belonging to the Homemakers Club. Although she had little time to cultivate leisure interests, Mom was easily able to visit friends and neighbors because she could drive a car.

Children First

Mom taught us that material things were not important. She did not collect items or possessions, and she did not believe that money brought happiness. She would rather have people and relationships than things.

Mom always felt it was more important for us kids to have a new Christmas or Easter outfit than for her to have new clothes herself. In eight years, Mom had only one new hat and one second-hand dress. She was always willing to go without so we kids did not have to.

God is not unjust; he will not forget your work and the love you have shown him as you have helped his people and continue to help them.
–Hebrews 6:10 (NIV)

CHAPTER 3

The Eight Ragamuffins

Family gave our lives meaning, structure, and stability. My parents and siblings provided unconditional love and acceptance. Everyone belonged, and everyone felt safe. We celebrated when someone soared and comforted each other when we faltered. We did not love our siblings more because they succeeded or less because they failed—we loved them the same no matter what.

Family life was a mixture of conversations, irritations, frustrations, celebrations, and negotiations. Unconditional love led us to expect and accept provocations from each other, so we learned to forgive each other a thousand times. Despite challenges and inevitable hurt feelings, we siblings became a close-knit, caring clan who loved each other regardless of our individual faults.

As brothers and sisters, we had a common history and a heritage of shared experiences that forged a unique bond between us. It was inevitable that we would band together since most of our interactions were with each other. We spent our days and nights together; we worked and played together; we ate together, celebrated holidays together, and went to school together. When we were not at school, our world consisted of the people living on the farm: the eight of us and our parents.

We enjoyed each other's company so much, it wasn't necessary to make other friends or pay for entertainment. All of us remember the joy of riding the swing in the haymow or playing kick the can on summer afternoons and how fun it was to spend winter days skating on the pond. We fondly recall the laughter provoked when we teased each other or how hard it was to fall asleep after hearing one of Daryl's funny stories.

Birth Order

A strong emphasis on self-sufficiency and hard work permeated our lives, and we were expected to contribute daily to the farm work. We older children were given considerable responsibilities at an early age. As major economic contributors, we knew we were indispensable, and we felt a great deal of pride. Most of the time Mom and Dad treated us as if we were adults, because they needed us to be.

Raised during a generation that socialized and educated children to a gender-based division of labor, my father considered "man's work" inappropriate for girls. However, blessed with an abundance of girls, he had no choice but to have his daughters provide the workforce for barn chores, hauling hay, picking rock, grinding feed, and numerous other farm duties. We girls spent our time performing a wide range of domestic tasks as well as handling barn and field chores. Our parents refused to show any favoritism—they appreciated and affirmed us all. They believed that women and men were equally intelligent and equally deserving of a fine education.

The Precocious Child: Warren

Warren, the firstborn child, was the intelligent and eccentric one. A precocious kid, his teachers said he displayed a photographic memory. We girls (the next three children born) accepted him as our opinionated and outspoken older brother, while he primarily considered us an aggravation.

Warren preferred to spend his time with a chemistry set, a microscope, or a book. One year for Christmas he received a Mr. Wizard Handy Andy Science Lab containing vials, bottles of chemicals, a candle, a compass, and magnets. We girls were his audience as he mixed chemicals to form smoke or foam. I remember him placing a hard-boiled egg over a bottle containing a burning piece of paper, and the egg fell into the bottle.

"Why does it do that?" Warren asked us girls, attempting to instruct us.

Continuing on, he asked us which egg would spin longer, a raw egg or a boiled egg. He poured two colorless fluids into a glass, and by the count of five, the fluid turned black.

"Why does it do that?" Warren asked again.

In the 1950s, a father aspired to have a son take over his farm. However, not being interested in farming, Warren challenged this idea. At age seven, he publicly affirmed his plan to attend college with no intention of following in his father and grandfather's farming footsteps. Nonetheless, as the only boy in the first half of the siblings, he worked as Dad's right-hand man and partner, cultivating fields twelve hours a day, pitching manure, and milking cows—but counting the years until he could escape the farm. Dad treated him as an equal, valuing the significance of his contributions and encouraging him with the promise of college.

Warren loved to argue, and since he did not want to waste intellectual energy on topics of importance with us girls, Dad became his debate partner, discussing politics or math equations. Warren loved puzzles and mind games, and he tried to define his own approach to solving any problem.

Three Peas in a Pod: Maxine, Audrey, and Jo

Born within a four-year span, we three sisters lived interdependently. We forged an unyielding bond, and we remain as close-knit today as we were in our youth. Sisterhood gave us a safe place to share and learn while still retaining our dignity. Each of us was willing to let insults pass, because our bonds were deeper than the width of our differences.

We spent our childhood working, playing, and going to school together. We shared confidences, created trouble, and confronted the world collectively. Given so many responsibilities at a young age, our environment shaped us to be self-reliant, independent risk takers rather than compliant and submissive. As much as we helped our mother over the years, I'm sure we drove her crazy, too.

To the community, we girls bore a striking resemblance: a little taller than most, a little thinner than average, dark-haired with bangs and the "bob" hairstyle, and clothes made by our grandma. We shared a common identity; we acted, talked, laughed, and thought alike; and we agreed on most issues. We often finished each other's sentences.

It was common to have conversations like this one with a store clerk: "You're Milton's oldest daughter?"

"No, I'm Audrey."

"Well," the clerk asked, "who is with you?"

"Jo is the next sister."

Shaking his head and smiling he said, "I can't tell you girls apart."

We had our not-so-nice moments, mostly devising schemes to provoke Warren because he owned a fine temper. When he settled into a chair with a book, we could not resist pounding out tunes on the piano, crooning the lyrics at top volume. We especially enjoyed practicing the song "Sisters," sung by Rosemary Clooney and Vera-Ellen in *White Christmas*.

Although we defined ourselves as "the girls," we each had a unique personality. Impulsive, fast-talking, fast-moving, and outgoing, I possessed a wild enthusiasm and flair for drama and storytelling. I delighted in cooking and protecting the younger kids. As the oldest sister, I was used to being in charge. I directed, or as Audrey and Jo said, *bossed,* in Mom's absence. Being the eldest daughter, I became the first to challenge my parents on various issues and often took the blame for the group. I heard a million times, "You're the oldest, and you should know better."

Audrey possessed Dad's gentle spirit. Easygoing and tenderhearted, she developed a passion for animals and preferred to work with the calves in the barn rather than work in the house. She did not care for competition, preferring to opt out of playing whist or board games. When she made up her mind about something, there was no changing it. She became a loyal friend to anyone she befriended.

Jo had a good head on her shoulders and was not afraid to think for herself and take risks. As the youngest of us three girls, she harmonized as an equal. Feisty and brassy, smart and not afraid to show it, her bold nature gave her permission to ignore conventions. Self-confident and assertive, Jo blossomed into a take-charge person, realizing big ideas and a penchant for freedom. Fun-loving and spontaneous, Jo grew to be competitive with a headstrong independence.

We spent our formative years taking care of four younger siblings; and, because we girls babysat at home, neighbors assumed we could also do it for them. At a very early age, we began babysitting on Wednesday nights (when the neighbors bowled) or on Saturday nights. We were asked often because others knew of our work ethic, as Mom insisted we do household chores (wash dishes and clean the house) while we were babysitting.

His Father's Son: Daryl

With a grin bursting from his dimpled, freckled, bright-eyed face and pockets bulging with nails, mud, bugs, and other treasures, four-year-old Daryl plopped himself under the tractor, watching and imitating Dad's actions.

"I think the front axle might need grease," Dad speculated.

"Yep, I think you're right," chimed in Daryl.

Crawling out from under the tractor, Dad pushed his cap back on his forehead and grabbed a blade of grass to chew on.

"That darn tractor is beyond repair," he sighed.

Daryl thrust his cap back and pulled a blade of grass to chew on, slid his hammer in his bib overalls, and said, "That's for sure."

Dad recognized his successor in his second son. Daryl trailed Dad from barn to shed, from pigpen to corncrib. He inspected the machinery, rode the tractor with Dad, and mimicked Dad's speech and mannerisms. Daryl went wherever Dad went. He helped with the milking chores, morning and night, and he rode with Dad to the creamery every day to help unload the cream cans.

Unique, curious, mischievous, and cute as a playful puppy, Daryl arrived as a breath of fresh air after three girls, and he endeared himself to everyone. A stocky little boy with a big imagination, he had a propensity for getting into trouble.

"Somebody flooded the water troughs in the barn," Dad said. "Does anyone know anything about it?"

"Oh, man, I saw Jake do it," replied Daryl as he put his head in his hands and shook his head.

"Your dog did it?" Dad asked.

"I saw him drinking out of one, and it got stuck," Daryl said. "And he didn't know how to 'unstuck' it, so he moved to the next one."

"I wonder if setting a trap at the bottom of each trough would keep a dog out," Dad suggested.

Daryl took a slow breath, "Oh . . . will it hurt him?"

"It will take his nose right off," said Dad.

"Oh, gosh, I'll tell him," said Daryl as he hung his head.

One day, as Daryl was on his way to bed, the sound of the metal cover on the cookie jar resonated through the kitchen.

"Daryl, come here," Mom said as Daryl tiptoed by. "Were you in the cookie jar?"

With his mouth full of cookies, he shook his head no and started to head upstairs.

"Oh, no, you don't, young man. Where do you think you're going? Get back here now," Mom commanded. "Were you in the cookie jar?"

"I can't remember," Daryl said with his head tilted down and his eyes looking up. He curled his nose and said, "I don't think so."

Taking a slow breath, Dad drummed his fingers on the table. "How many did you take?"

"One."

"Impossible," Dad gave him a disbelieving look. "Let me see what's in your pocket."

"They must have fallen in when I took one cookie," Daryl said with a puzzled frown as he pulled three cookies out of his pocket and set them on the table. "Sorry," Daryl sniffled, rubbing his eyes and waddling upstairs. "Dad, call me when you wake up. I want to feed our new calves."

"I don't know why, but I can't be angry at him," Mom said.

"I know what you mean. He has a heart of gold," Dad replied with a big grin.

"Of course, he is you with that puppy dog face," Mom said.

"You've got that right." Dad laughed.

The Little Footprints: Eydie, Dave, and Diane

As constant as seasons, as recurrent as a rising sun, our home welcomed a new brother or sister every two years, and each new sibling was an added joy. Born in the hospital in Fergus Falls, each baby came home in a new receiving blanket. I slept in the east parlor downstairs for a couple weeks for the last two arrivals. I changed and fed them when they woke up during the night so Mom could get some sleep. We older girls formed a powerful emotional attachment to our youngest siblings. We liked watching the little kids because they were cute and funny and, like baby puppies, they were playful, mischievous, and fun to cuddle. We girls were often the first ones there when they learned to crawl, pulled themselves up on the couch, lost their first tooth, said their first word, and took their first steps.

Even our Shetland pony, Sandy, helped care for the little ones. On washdays when everyone was busy, we propped two of the youngest on Sandy's back, and she walked around and around the house, giving them a ride. When she tired of it, Sandy would wander to the front hill, lower her neck, and bump the children off. Nobody ever got hurt, and the little ones found something else to do while Sandy headed for the barn.

We older siblings were the fiercest protectors of our brothers and sisters. Mom was still the disciplinarian, and she set their boundaries and expectations. But of course, the little ones ran to one of us girls after they received a scolding.

Children are a heritage from the LORD,
offspring a reward from him.
–Psalm 127:3 (NIV)

Grandma Galena

CHAPTER 4

Grandma Galena

The grandchildren of Norwegian settlers, my grandparents lived their entire lives in or near Dalton, where they attended church and did their shopping. Grandpa, a World War I veteran, and Grandma raised four sons on the farm. When they retired from farming, they moved to Dalton, and my father took over the farm. Grandpa continued to work in town, serving as temporary postmaster and county surveyor until his death at the age of sixty-five.

With Norwegian as their first language, my grandparents spoke English with a Scandinavian accent. Common for Norwegians, they struggled to pronounce the letters "J" and "W," especially at the beginning of a word, and their sentences frequently ended with "then" or "you know." Years later, we grandchildren recognized that our own language also contained these colloquialisms.

Town living suited Grandma. After Grandpa died, Grandma lived alone for more than two decades in her small house in

Dalton. I am sure she missed Grandpa, who, according to many (including my Mom), was the kindest person they had ever met. Yet Grandma did not allow herself to wallow in loneliness. She chose to enjoy life. Church socials, coffee get-togethers, card parties, weddings, birthdays, grandchildren, and even funerals filled her calendar and kept her socially active. Her siblings all lived in or near Dalton, too.

Grandma's animated sense of humor, unconditional kindness, and gregarious personality drew people to her. Strong and independent, she kept busy and contributed to society with her sewing, quilting, needlework, and hospitality. She was quick on her feet and fast with her hands. She never, in her entire life, wore slacks or drove a car.

Grandma's House

Grandma Galena lived in a small house in Dalton across the street from the school. We dropped in to say hello and have a cookie almost every day, and Dad went by frequently to enjoy coffee with her. My memories of those times are wonderful ones.

Two big arborvitaes graced the entrance to Grandma's house. Even though her home was small, it was like a castle to us kids. It had wall-to-wall carpeting, French doors, a basement, and a bathroom with a tub, sink, and flushing stool—all things we did not have on the farm. It also had hot-water heat registers, which required no wood, and a laundry chute, which amazed us kids to no end. Grandma had a china hutch filled with beautiful cups and saucers, a lovely hurricane lamp, and wonderful photo albums of times past. The upstairs seemed dark and scary to me, but we never slept up there. It consisted of two windowless rooms—an attic space and a large open bedroom, which was used mostly as a storage room. There was a crawl space, which I found very suspicious, between the attic and the bedroom. Even Grandma didn't go upstairs more than a couple times a year.

Our Second Home

Grandma's house was our second home. On the days we did not ride our bikes to school, Dad collected us after school at Grandma's house. As soon as school let out, we hustled across the street. Running up the steps and bursting through Grandma's front door, we crossed through the living room to the kitchen. Grandma treated us to cookies or donuts while we recounted our day at school.

Dad brought Grandma cream, milk, butter, eggs, or meat from the farm and delivered her mail to her. A typical conversation between them went something like this: "Is anyone home? Are you here, Ma?" Dad would call as he entered the foyer.

Grandma would appear in the kitchen door, wiping her hands on her apron with a big grin. "So, then, it's you, Milton. You have time for lunch, don't you?"

"Don't go to any trouble," Dad would say as he sat in a kitchen chair.

"*Nei da*, it's no trouble, you know." Sometimes Dad and Grandma spoke English, sometimes they spoke Norwegian, and sometimes a little of both.

Overnights with Grandma

"Well, time to get going. We have chores to do," Dad would say, after determining which one of us kids could stay with Grandma. She let one grandchild stay overnight with her each night.

I so loved when it was my night to stay in town. Grandma lavished me with undivided attention, and taking a bubble bath in her real bathtub was a luxury we did not have on the farm. We kids would run errands for her, walking the two blocks downtown to purchase groceries, fabric, rickrack, thread, buttons, or muslin for a quilt. "Dicker for the best deal then," she told us as we left. "And buy yourself a candy bar or ice cream cone, you know."

"*Mange takk,*" we said, thanking her.

Grandma had been blessed with four wonderful sons (my dad was her second) but no daughters. So when her granddaughters came along, she was delighted to have girls to sew for, take to mother/daughter banquets at church, and to dote on. We girls had a special bond with Grandma, and I treasured the time I spent with her.

After supper, Grandma would gather her latest *McCall's* magazine and a scissor, turning to the Betsy McCall paper doll page. Grandma read the story to me, and I cut out the Betsy paper doll and her beautiful clothing.

These were the evenings when Grandma taught me to embroider days-of-the-week dishtowels made from white flour sacks. Together we selected colors from Grandma's vast array of embroidery threads. Grandma would iron on a transfer, and—thimbles in place and embroidery hoops in hand—we would begin stitching. She bleached flour sacks, hemmed them, and guided us as we embroidered on them to make kitchen towels. She also taught me to embroider dresser scarves, knit bedroom slippers, and crochet doilies.

As we did needlework together, we embarked on long, lazy conversations. Grandma told me about her four sons being born on the farm. She talked of her husband and sons joining the armed forces. She spoke of rationing sugar and coffee during the war. She laughed when she told me that in 1922, when she was twenty-two years old, the 19th Amendment to the United States

Constitution granted women the right to vote. Through our conversations, Grandma became a strong influence on my thinking.

Artistic Flair

Grandma never owned an electric sewing machine. Hers was a cabinet-mounted treadle machine with a foot pedal. While Grandma pumped with her feet, she used both hands to manipulate the fabric as the treadle powered her belt-driven sewing machine. The faster she pumped, the faster she sewed.

Grandma expressed her creativity and displayed her artistic flair through needlework. Sewing was her gift for family and friends. She crocheted beautiful doilies and tablecloths, embroidered dishtowels and dresser scarves, tatted beautiful hardanger edges on pillowcases and tablecloths, cross-stitched gingham aprons, knitted booties, and stitched hankies; and she delighted in sewing dresses, jumpers, and blouses for her granddaughters.

Quilting Bees

A close-knit group of Grandma's friends, all accomplished quilters, went from house to house during the winter months, engaging in quilting bees. This group of women, including Grandma, had the creativity, patience, and skill to honor this folk art. Possessing an excellent eye for design, Grandma assembled coordinating fabric scraps of different colors and patterns into quilting blocks. These blocks were joined together to make the quilt top. Her favorite quilt designs included the Dresden Plate, Double Wedding Ring, Fan, and Log Cabin. She hand-pieced blocks as she turned under raw outside edges, ironed, and basted. When a grandchild left for college or got married, they received a beautiful quilt from Grandma.

Many afternoons, Grandma sat around a large quilting frame with her friends Alma, Florence, Ruth, Hulda, and Lillian. Wearing silver thimbles on their third fingers, they quilted from the center outward. With precision, they cut thread, passed it through a needle, and made a simple small knot at the end of thread. Each quilter pulled her thread through the material, gave a gentle tug, and brought the needle up as she kept to six stitches on the needle at one time.

Concentrating on the work before them did not deter them from storytelling, laughter, and conversation. Grandma and her friends had many folksy sayings such as "*uff da*," "okay then," "just a sliver," "you bet," and "you shouldn't have." When they quilted, their tongues went as fast as their hands.

Egg Coffee and Afternoon Lunch

Norwegian heritage dictated serving afternoon lunch and strong coffee. In the middle of the table, Grandma placed a pitcher of cream, a bowl of Domino sugar cubes, open-face cheese sandwiches, and cookies. She served strong coffee using her cup-and-saucer sets in various flower patterns. Holding a small strainer over each cup, she poured the coffee and strained out the grounds. After adding cream, each woman dunked a sugar cube in their coffee, sucked out the sweetness, and then added the cube to their coffee. Grandma and her friends poured their coffee into their saucers to cool before tipping the saucers to their lips.

Grandma's Legacy

Grandma's impact on our family was greater than anyone could have imagined. She left many wonderful memories in my mind and heart, and my life has been richer because she was such a huge part of my childhood.

Grandma's face is etched in my mind as clear as a bright summer day. I can still see those warm eyes and hear her quick wit. I recall her curly steel-gray hair, her smiling face so full of character. Most of all, her gentleness was evident to all.

When I was at Grandma's house, I was the star. Grandma was always telling me how proud she was of me, and she was excited to hear about everything I was doing. I will always cherish those memories.

But the fruit of the Spirit is love, joy, peace, forbearance,
kindness, goodness, faithfulness, gentleness, self-control. . .
–Galatians 5:22,23 (NIV)

PART TWO

Home

The Home Place 1949

CHAPTER 5

The Home Place

Few things resonate as deeply within me as thoughts of my childhood home. Our farmstead, which encompassed 280 acres, included lush green pastures, a twenty-acre pond, fields of rippling wheat and oats, and scattered maple, oak, linden, and ash groves. Picturesque and serene, our farm was nestled in scenic rolling Midwest farmland two miles south of the village of Dalton.

High lines followed winding gravel roads, pastures were enclosed by barbed wire and electric fences, and a long gravel driveway led visitors to the house. A concrete silo attached to a red wooden barn with white trim and a cupola indicated a dairy operation. Other structures included a two-story granary, a large machine shed with a pig shed underneath, a gas barrel, an open-slated corncrib, a tool shed, a brooder house, and an outhouse. A yard light with a rain gauge attached glowed between the house and the barn. Twenty feet behind our house stood a vacant smokehouse that Grandma and Grandpa had used to smoke ham and bacon.

The home itself, which occupied a hill overlooking the farm, was a stately two-story white wood-frame house built in 1900 by Dad's grandfather, Cornelius Erickson. The house was embellished with ornate Victorian gables on three sides, pine shingles, a good many windows, and three welcoming porches. The dining room and living room doors opened onto a wraparound screened-in porch. However, it was the two porches off the kitchen that visitors and family used. The north porch contained a small room we called a shanty, which was filled with wood for the kitchen stove, while the second porch faced south, allowing summer breezes to waft from one porch through to the next, cooling the kitchen. A stand of apple and plum trees, a vegetable garden, and a showy lilac hedge surrounded the extensive yard. On the north side, a five-acre hardwood grove sheltered our home from winter's penetrating winds. A sloping front yard provided a perfect location for children to slide down. Beyond the front yard was a magnificent tapestry of pastureland, meadows, and rolling fields.

Heart of the Home: The Kitchen

The kitchen thrived as the center of family activity. A large table graced the middle of the room, where we gathered to eat meals, play cards, share a cup of coffee with neighbors, finish homework, or challenge family members to a board game. Anyone entering or leaving the house came through one of the two kitchen porches. A knock indicated visitors, and the slam of a wooden screen door signaled a family member. In the winter, we continually heard Mom say, "Shut the door—we're not heating the outside. Were you born in a barn?"

The inviting smells of pies or homemade bread floated

from the oven, and a small radio played uninterrupted. Besides Mom's much-loved music, the kitchen radio provided us with weather forecasts, local news, and hospital reports. At 11:30, Mom caught the market reports. She kept Dad informed of how barrows and gilts were doing on the market as well as steers and heifers.

A bank calendar containing monthly pockets for receipts and sales expenses hung on the north wall. The shelves above the sink collected letters, arrowheads, and keys. A practical breadbox and metal canisters sat on the linoleum countertop, and a built-in flour bin housed a fifty-pound sack of flour. Into the junk drawer we tossed pencils, erasers, paper, scissors, and anything else needing a home. Flypaper strips hung from the ceiling with dead flies stuck to the paper spirals. I thought the strips were disgusting, along with the fly swatter Mom kept around for the same purpose.

A long narrow pantry with floor-to-ceiling shelves on the back wall served as a coatroom and a place to store food. Coat hooks for each member of the family lined a wall in the pantry, and boots were neatly arranged below them. This was where the washtub was set up for Saturday night baths.

A Place of Grace: The Dining Room

The large dining room, the center room in our house, contained a huge bay window that faced the front lawn and an east door leading to the living room. In summer, Mom kept the shades down in the living and dining rooms to create a cool sanctuary. Lacy starched curtains, a bronze globed chandelier, eight chairs around a long oak table, and a matching china hutch filled the dining room, while a shiny-waxed flowered linoleum floor and white plaster walls gave it grace. Fragrant peonies, with beautiful red, pink, and white petals, or sweet-smelling lilacs adorned the table in summer. An oil-burning stove added heat during winter. We ate Sunday dinner in the dining room, using a white damask tablecloth and our fine china and silver.

A trap door in the dining room floor led down to a cement-walled cellar with a dirt floor, while an outside stoop provided a summertime entrance. I hated going into the dark, creepy cellar because slimy yellow salamanders lived under the steps. Rows of canned fruits and vegetables in Mason jars lined shelves along the walls; and potatoes, carrots, and squash filled several gunnysacks.

The Living Room or Front Parlor

Crossing the dining room, we entered our living room or, as Grandma called it, our front parlor. Mom and Dad also called it the east room. Brown flowered linoleum and stucco walls complemented the venetian blinds and floral drapes. The room was furnished with a davenport, Dad's rocking chair, a standing ashtray, armchairs, our prized *World Book Encyclopedias*, and a phonograph player. An upright piano, out of tune and with some keys unplayable, stood against the wall. Crocheted doilies from Grandma Galena graced the end tables. Outside doors from the dining room and living room led to a large screened-in porch. Perhaps this porch was meant to be the entrance to the house, but we never used it for that purpose. For us, the two kitchen porches served as the main entrances to the house.

The Master Bedroom

Entering my parents' small sleeping quarters off the dining room, the first thing to notice was the smell of baby oil and baby powder. This was because the newest baby always occupied a crib in this room. A wooden crucifix with palm fronds tucked behind it hung over my parents' bed. Once a year, on Palm Sunday, my mother would change the fronds she received at mass. The small walk-in closet was where Mom always hid our Christmas presents.

Keeping Us Warm: The Wood-burning Stove

A coal- and wood-burning cast-iron cookstove provided the main source of heat for the house. It allowed heat to escape upstairs when the door remained open. Small strips of kindling were placed inside the firebox with paper to start a fire. After the kindling was burning well, we added larger pieces of wood by placing a handle into a groove on the round plates and throwing the wood in.

We girls carried wood in from the shanty to stack alongside the stove. Since the wood always needed replenishing, carrying wood from the woodpile to the shanty was a job we kids did every day. When it was cold outside, we kept the stove going from morning until night. And before we went to bed, Mom or Dad banked the fire. When I was around eleven, we got a gas stove that used propane tanks.

Running Water: The Cistern, Kitchen, and Bathroom

The kitchen sink was the only source of running water in the house. It served as both the place where we cleaned the dishes and the washbasin where we all gathered to brush our teeth, wash our hands, and give the babies a bath. Drinking water came from a drilled well with a mechanical pump that moved the water, but a cistern supplied the nice soft water for everything else. A trap door in the kitchen floor led to the cistern, and a downspout pipe directed rainwater from the roof into the cistern. A second pipe was used for pumping water out of the cistern into the house. The cistern pump was located under the kitchen cabinets, while the well pump was located in the cellar. It seemed that in winter it was a constant struggle to keep the water lines from freezing.

Toothbrushes amassed in a small mirrored medicine cabinet on the wall near the kitchen sink, a towel holder on the wall held our towels, and we placed our shared combs and brushes in a drawer. The big galvanized tub used on laundry day became our bathtub on Saturday nights. We girls bathed first, followed by the little kids, and finally the boys. In summer, the lake became our bathtub. Mom and Dad did not add a bathroom to the house until after the seventh child was born (at which point I was in high school). I guess they never really saw a need for it until then.

A wooden outhouse, located a respectable distance from our house, served as the bathroom, with newspapers and magazine pages used for toilet paper. Our outhouse had a half-moon opening in the door, additional small ventilation openings on both sidewalls, and three large open seats. In the freezing winter, we stayed inside and used a portable potty in the unheated attic.

Party Line: The Telephone

Our telephone hung by the front door. We were on a party line, which meant that one or more other families also used the same line. We shared a party line with six other farms. Our signal was a long, two shorts, and a long. In those days, relatives often lived close to each other, so grandparents or a great aunt might be on the same line. Knowing that others listened in on their calls, Alma and Grandma talked in Norwegian so younger ears could not understand what they said. Neighbors on the party line could also listen in on your call if they had a mind to. If someone was talking when we wanted to make a call, we just had to wait our turn unless it was an emergency, at which point we could ask to break in. Long-distance calls were so expensive that Mom and Dad made them only in dire emergencies.

The Rooms Upstairs

Ascending a steep wooden staircase off the kitchen, we entered a huge hall with spindle railings enclosing a staircase. Although designated as a playroom, we seldom used it since we played outside in summer and the room was not heated in winter. We ran races around the staircase and straddled the railings to perform "dangerous" feats. The large room-sized hall housed our few toys, a wooden cupboard, and a doll bed. It also contained Mom and Dad's home library, comprised of *Reader's Digest* books.

The upstairs hallway led to three bedrooms, an unfinished walk-in attic, and a closet. These rooms were decorated with painted plank floors, rugs, and sheer curtains on the windows. Each bedroom was furnished with a dresser and an iron-framed bed covered with a chenille bedspread. Dirty clothes were placed in the corner behind the door until washday, when we threw them down the stairway.

The upstairs was unheated, except for the little heat that escaped through a small grate above the dining room stove. On cold winter nights, our parents left the kitchen door ajar to allow extra heat to travel upstairs, and we kept our bedroom doors open to let in the extra bit of warmth. We wore heavy flannel pajamas and slept beneath multiple blankets to ward off chills. In winter, frost covered the windows so we could not see out, and when the windows rattled during a blizzard we buried ourselves deep under several handmade quilts. In the mornings, we dressed on the iron grille register or grabbed our clothes and headed downstairs to dress by the oil stove. My memories of winter always include a howling wind trying to get in through the windows.

Mom's cedar hope chest and an old trunk from Norway rested in the big east bedroom upstairs. Mom was raised during a generation when it was common for unmarried women to put together a trousseau of household goods that would serve her well when she got married. Traditionally, it included items such as linens, kitchenware, crockery, sewing notions, and bedding. Her hope chest was always kind of a mystery, because she kept it locked.

A large trap door in the hall ceiling led to an attic we never entered. When we asked Dad what was up there, he said he did not know. To us kids, this mysterious room sparked our imagination for all manner of stories.

Another door led to a walk-in attic that was filled with seasonal and hand-me-down clothes, Christmas tree ornaments, and used Christmas wrapping paper. During the winter months, a portable toilet was set up in the attic for emergencies. Little brown bats hung upside-down in the cobwebbed darkness, and if someone left this door ajar the bats swooped into the hallway at night. Seeing a dark shape glide through the air or cling to a wall, we screamed and hid under our quilts until Dad came upstairs with the kitchen broom to kill the poor creature.

"They eat our mosquitoes and aren't interested in human blood," Dad would say.

"For crying out loud, Milton, bats carry rabies and bite people," Mom would reply, standing at the bottom of the stairs with her hands on her hips. "Rabies shots are a foot long, and you have to take them in the stomach." We girls learned to fear what Mom feared.

Home Improvements

Every fall when the last crops were in, our family made a few purchases. Investments in machinery were always the first priority. Most of the money went for farm equipment or repairs or occasionally a different car, but some of it would be spent on school clothes and updating the house. A bathroom was installed after the seventh child was born. Central heating was not added until after I had left for college.

Gradually, the house received a new kitchen stove, a black-and-white television, an electric mixer, and finally a clothes dryer for the countless diapers. Items such as a deep freeze, vacuum cleaner (we only had linoleum floors), a washing machine, and a furnace were not added until after I left home.

My people will live in peaceful dwelling places,
in secure homes, in undisturbed places of rest.
–Isaiah 32:18 (NIV)

CHAPTER 6

A Symphony of Seasons

One of my favorite songs is "What a Wonderful World," sung by the late Louis Armstrong. The way he sings about nature, babies being born, and neighbors saying "hi" resonates deeply with me and still evokes feelings and memories from my years spent growing up on the farm. *"I see trees of green, red roses, too. I see them bloom for me and for you, and I think to myself, what a wonderful world . . ."*

What a wonderful world indeed. The sophistication of a crimson shrub rose in our front yard, the strength of a grand oak tree . . . these were just two examples of nature's vast beauty that we witnessed all around us. The color of the sky as we lay on our backs in the soft grass and deciphered shapes in the clouds made the farmstead a wonderful world to all of us kids.

Nature was vitally important to a Midwest farm family. For us, it was imperative that nature bless us with good weather to grow our crops. The color of the sky at morning and night was a sign as to whether conditions were conducive for fieldwork. For Dad, understanding nature was crucial to survival.

A Sense of Place

Life on the farm forged in us a powerful bond with the four diverse seasons that colored our natural world. A sense of place emerged as I heard the crashes of summer thunder, the howl of a winter storm, or the rustle of fallen leaves. The sense of place deepened as I felt the harsh fury of a winter blizzard, witnessed the melting snow of spring, and endured the brutal heat of summer. We enjoyed the smell of lilacs in the spring and of burning leaves in the fall. We frolicked joyfully in the summer months and warmed our frozen toes in winter.

Farm chores were framed by the four seasons: picking rock in spring, hauling hay in summer, harvesting corn in fall, and digging silage in winter. Play varied by the four seasons, too: In the summer we swam, in autumn we took hayrides, and in winter we went sledding.

Signs of Spring

Occasionally spring burst forth in late March, but most years it arrived in April. Mounds of snow began to melt, sending cascading water to the pond. A ravine in the north woods filled with torrents of rushing water, which tumbled frothily into the pond, giving us unlimited new diversions for play. We made dams and let the water fill up behind them before it spilled over to make a waterfall.

Spring was really like two seasons. The first half was the thawing season, also called the mud season. When the snow melted in the barnyard and patches of bare ground opened up, one of us was sure to lose a rubber boot. We wore our overshoes in spring, so we were free to jump in puddles and make great splashes. Dad said spring arrived when he smelled the indigenous earth again, and he began preparing the soil for planting.

The second half of spring was a beautiful awakening. Days began with a morning chorus of birdsongs. The male cardinal, a year-round bird, perched high on a limb and called for a female to come to his territory. The crows, which stayed around all winter, seemed to make more noise than usual. Geese formations pointed north, their distant honking signaling their course. We heard meadowlarks and saw the flash of the redwing blackbird's brilliant sash. On the barn roof, pigeons cooed in tones as soft as velvet. Mom said the harbinger of spring is when you notice the first robin hopping across the lawn in search of earthworms.

For two weeks in May, lilac shrubs produced an array of dark purple, lavender, and white clusters, while their sweet scent filled the soft morning air. Grandma said Scandinavian homesteaders planted lilacs around their houses because they were one of the few flowering shrubs that survived the Minnesota winters.

Bright yellow dandelions peppered our farm in late April, turning into white seed heads overnight. The beautiful heart-shaped flowers of the bleeding hearts burst forth, as did the delicate columbine flower, enticing the hummingbirds to feed. The red shoots of peonies pushed through the ground; tulips and daffodils erupted and flowered; and crocus corms sprouted under the trees, enticing rabbits to nibble on their tasty flowers and buds.

Images of Summer

To us kids, summer was June, July, and August—the months we were out of school—although Warren said it did not officially start until June 20 or 21, a time called the summer solstice. By June, our farm was an emerald playground where we enjoyed unbridled exploration around fields, pastures, and woodland. Leaves graced the maple, ash, linden, and box elder trees. Intoxicating scents of fresh-cut alfalfa and grass filled the air.

Riding our bikes to town in June, we observed painted turtles crossing the road. Warren said they were females moving from the slough to dry land to lay their eggs. From the intricate industry of the anthills to the playful chattering of chipmunks to the muskrat lodges on the pond, the animal kingdom was alive and active.

Our natural environment offered many playgrounds: the yard, woods, pasture, garden, and the pond. We climbed trees and built playhouses in the woods. We were constantly on a treasure hunt for animal tracks, feathers, rocks, and berries. Meandering through the flowerbeds, we plucked sticky petunias, inhaled the heady fragrant scent of sweet peas pushing skyward on a wire trellis, and detected hints of yellow in the violet irises. Bees buzzed in the salvia, balmy lilies whispered in the gentle breeze, and warm marigolds released an invigorating scent. We popped periwinkle balloon flowers and peeled the orange paper husks on Chinese lanterns, rupturing the tiny tomato berries containing a million seeds.

Summer brought gardens bursting with color. The bridal wreath spireas bloomed in June, and crispy paper hollyhocks stretched to the sky. By July, the five-foot tall pink Rugosa shrub roses were in full bloom, and we delighted in their glorious fragrance and beauty.

Rain, lightning, thunder, and hail visited us intermittently throughout the summer. A late-afternoon thunderstorm started with distant rumbling, a darkening sky, and a sudden howling wind. Within a few minutes, Mom hollered at us to hurry into the house and shut the windows upstairs. If she feared a tornado, she opened the cellar door. With our eyes peeled out the windows, we shuddered at the percussive crashes as strong winds tossed tree-tops back and forth while torrents of rain crashed down. Lightning flashes lit the darkened sky, followed by cracks of thunder. When the storm ended, a beautiful rainbow appeared above the rolling wheat fields.

Following a sky aflame at sunset, we counted stars as they emerged and identified constellations. Nights were never quiet: grasshoppers and crickets chirped, and frogs called back and forth to one another. Lightning bugs danced in the dark. We caught them in jars and then set them free.

Summer was the time for cultivating cornfields—waiting to see if our corn would be "knee-high by the Fourth of July"—hauling hay, and harvesting grain.

Harvest Moon

The fall season started on the first day back to school in September and lasted until mid-November when the snow came. Autumn signaled cooler temperatures, frost on the morning ground, bonfires, Halloween, jack-o-lanterns, hayrides, corn picking, hunting, and the sound of crunching leaves as we walked through the woods.

In autumn, nature painted a blazing work of art. Sugar maples turned brick red, ash trees glowed orange and yellow; and oak trees stood proud as they dropped acorns, keeping their golden brown leaves until March. Blazing sumac and deep-yellow box elder leaves fell in disarray, blanketing the ground. Grandma and Mom delighted in the dazzling show of copper and rust mums, purple asters, lemon yellow marigolds, bronze goldenrod, and a rainbow of dahlias.

Diligent squirrels and chattering chipmunks stored nuts and acorns, geese honked while hastening south in V-formations, frogs burrowed in the slough's mud bottom, and monarch butterflies filled up on milkweed before departing for Mexico. Honeybees clustered on sedum before the frost ended their feast.

Dad relished pheasant, duck, and deer hunting in autumn, but mostly he loved the accomplishment of a final harvest. To him, autumn grandeur was a field of ripe corn ready for harvest, the heavy-laden stalks glowing in the autumn sun, the music of the wind sweeping across the golden tassels. Dad chopped field corn into silage, picked ear corn, and then plowed the fields to get them ready for spring.

Winter Wonderland

The first snowfall usually arrived in November, and the excitement it caused is hard to explain. If we were in school, the teachers might let us out for recess. If we were at home, we ran outside the minute we were done with our chores.

Winter was a season of sledding, ice skating, ice fishing, fox and geese, king of the hill, snowball fights, building forts, and digging tunnels. Winter was also a season of fierce blizzards, several feet of snow, Alberta clippers, and subzero temperatures. Winter was Christmas.

As I walked to the house in the moonlit snow after completing my chores, I often lingered as I enjoyed the sight of the clear night sky and the sound of snow crunching beneath my feet. The stars were so close and bright, I almost felt I could touch them.

Winter nights were often filled with an eerie silence.

On another night, I might have to walk backward to get some relief from the wind that whipped with such ferocity I had a hard time catching my breath. I would hurry as fast as I could back to the house, where I knew a warm wood fire would be burning in the kitchen stove.

The Blizzard of 1957

Shrill north winds whipped across barren fields, and snow blanketed our farm. As winds howled and temperatures dropped, Dad seemed to know an arctic storm was coming and instructed us kids to fetch an extra armful of wood from the woodpile. We learned to recognize worsening weather.

Mom listened to the weather forecast: "Thirty-five-mile-per-hour winds, with accumulations of ten to fifteen inches of snow possible, and a wind chill of 30 below. Blowing and drifting snow is expected to cause whiteout conditions and to continue tonight and tomorrow."

We kids knew a whiteout meant no school and being stranded for several days. Dad, being the school board chair, would call board members to decide if they should cancel school. A raging winter blizzard was an adventure. Snuggled in bed with my sisters, we listened to howling winds rattle the windows, safe and secure in our house with a wood-burning stove to keep us warm.

With this particular storm, winds gusting at 40 miles an hour caused a hazardous whiteout with a wind chill below zero. Heavy snow and blowing winds formed large drifts around the buildings on our property and across the path to the barn. We scratched through frost on the windows to watch the whirling snow.

It seemed a storm summoned untapped energy and camaraderie in our family. We had to finish our barn chores before the power lines failed. The livestock needed food and water regardless of weather conditions. We had to keep the pipes from freezing in the house and the barn, so we left the kitchen sink water trickling all day.

Without warning, around eleven o'clock in the morning, the electric and telephone lines snapped. Although we lost electricity and phone service, our wood-burning stove provided heat and meals. Dad used a standby generator, powered by a tractor, to supply power to the barn during power outages to milk the cows.

Later that evening, the lights flickered several times before returning. Wind howled all night as gusts of 50 to 60 miles per hour drove heavy snow on top of what had fallen earlier. Around noon the third day, the wind finally stopped. By late afternoon, Dad used a tractor to clear the road, making huge ten-foot snow banks. We were thrilled to get out and play, knowing hot cocoa would be waiting for us when we went back inside.

We repeated stories of the storm for years. "Remember the 1957 storm? Never seen anything like it. Snow so deep we couldn't find the barn." Over time, the stories became so embellished we did not know reality from fantasy, but we all enjoyed recounting our grand adventures.

A Time for Everything

No place on earth is the cycle of life as evident as in the country. Nothing remains the same. Nothing remains forever. Wise King Solomon understood the farm season when he wrote:

There is a time for everything,
and a season for every activity under the heavens:
a time to be born and a time to die,
a time to plant and a time to uproot,
a time to kill and a time to heal,
a time to tear down and a time to build,
a time to weep and a time to laugh,
a time to mourn and a time to dance,
a time to scatter stones and a time to gather them,
a time to embrace and a time to refrain from embracing,
a time to search and a time to give up,
a time to keep and a time to throw away,
a time to tear and a time to mend,
a time to be silent and a time to speak,
a time to love and a time to hate,
a time for war and a time for peace.
–Ecclesiastes 3:1–8 (NIV)

PART THREE

Work

Raggamuffins

CHAPTER 7

Barn Chores

Work Ethic

As a child, I was taught that work never hurt anybody—thus the reason for rising at 6:30 a.m. to help with the barn chores. Farm kids were morning kids; never during my childhood did any one of us sleep past our standard wake-up time. Barn chores were a continuous cycle, yet specific tasks varied from summer to winter. Twice a day, Dad milked about twenty Holsteins while we kids fed the cows, pigs, and chickens. Helping with chores to the best of our ability was critical for running the farm. Even the little ones could throw corn over a fence to pigs, haul grain in a little red wagon, or open and shut the gate while Dad hauled manure.

As challenging as summer chores could be, winter chores were even more difficult. During the winter, we did barn chores in the morning before school and then again after school. We dug silage before we ate dinner at 5:00 and returned to the barn at 6:00

to feed the calves and throw down hay. Thankfully, even when the outside temperature dipped below zero, the inside of the barn stayed warm from the heat of the animals.

Digging Silage

One of the toughest chores was digging silage. To this day, I can see and smell the fermented silage, and I can feel my frozen toes as we worked. After school on winter afternoons, two of us, wearing buckled overshoes and caps with earflaps, climbed the forty-foot silo chute. My breath raced as I clasped the steel rungs to reach the top. Crawling through the door, I shivered at the frigid temperature in the silo and rubbed my hands before I grabbed a pitchfork and began tossing silage down the chute I had just climbed. Dad would have loosened the frozen silage with a pick-axe earlier in the afternoon. We kids pitched silage in front of the chute door until a substantial pile accumulated; then we pitched it to the silo room (the small room at the bottom of the silo chute). Through vapors of breath, we played word games or discussed Warren's theories while working:

"What is the largest number?"

"What comes after a zillion?"

"How long would it take you to count to a million?"

After what seemed like an eternity, when the bottom pile reached a certain height, Dad hollered, "That's enough." I climbed down until I was close enough to jump into the mound at the bottom. Our next chore was to carry silage by galvanized tubs to the manger. The warmth of the snug barn was heavenly after our claustrophobic time in the sub-zero silo.

Milking the Cows

As cows filed into the barn and entered their stalls to eat silage and drink from their individual drinking cups, we closed the wood and metal stanchions. The soft rhythm of machines pumping milk, and cows chewing along to country tunes drifting from the radio, made the warm barn a pleasant place to work. Dad's jovial demeanor made these chores even more agreeable.

The Holsteins trusted Dad's touch and calm voice as he sat on an overturned bucket between two cows and attached four suction cups to each cow, always wary of being stepped on or swatted by a tail. When the milk bucket was full, Dad carried it to the sterile milk room and poured the warm milk into a large container on top of the DeLaval separator. That machine swirled the liquid around, separating the cream and milk before pouring them out separate spouts to be collected in tall milk cans and short cream cans that were placed in a coldwater tank for Dad to haul to the creamery in the morning.

Shortly after any calves were born, Dad moved them into a pen where we kids taught them to drink warm milk from a bucket. First we got the calf to suck on our fingers and then we dipped our hand into the bucket of warm milk. The calves greedily snorted milk out of their noses, butted the milk pails, and wedged our fingers in the pails. Soon they learned to drink on their own. Then they moved to a drink we made by mixing warm water with a powdery milk replacer—it had such a strong smell. I'll never forget it.

Fun with Language and Math

Between chores, we rallied around a wooden bench that Dad rested on while the cows milked. Dad taught us to count and to say the days of week in Norwegian. *En, to, tre, fire, fem, seks, sju, ate, in,* and *ti* are the words for counting one to ten. The days of the week are "*Mandag, Tirsdag, Onsdag, Torsdag, Fredag, Lordag,* and *Sondag.* Mostly, Dad engaged us in math challenges.

"If a train goes 150 miles in three hours, how many miles did it go in four hours?"

"Hilmer is eight years older than his sister. In three years, he will be twice as old as she is. How old are they now?"

"In three hours the temperature dropped eight degrees. How many degrees did the temperature drop per hour?"

"Here's one, Daryl. If I gave you two dimes, four nickels, and five pennies, how much money did I give you?"

"Warren, the product of the ages of three brothers is 72seventy-two, and the sum of their ages is a number greater than 100. What are their ages?"

Hayloft at Night

Throughout the winter, we dragged round hay bales out of the dim, cold hayloft to the manger, bale by bale, using only our body strength and bale hooks. Once in the manger, we cut the twine, unrolled the bales, and spread them out for the cows to eat. What made getting the hay bales difficult was that, when we loaded the haymow in the summer, we let the bales fall off the elevator randomly and did not stack them. This made playing in the haymow lots of fun, but also made it harder to pull bales out in the winter. We ended this task by cleaning the hay out of the cows' drinking cups with our hands. Then we pitched straw bales down a chute that Dad spread out for bedding for the animals.

Grinding Feed

During the winter, grinding feed was a constant Saturday afternoon ritual that none of us four oldest were exempt from. No matter how low the temperature dropped, we ground a week's supply of corn. A long belt attached to a tractor ran a feed grinder. One kid sat on the tractor and held in the brake, knowing that if he or she released the brake on the Allis Chalmers it would slack the belt drive and the grinder would stop. With legs barely long enough to reach the pedals, we slid off the seat as far as possible to reach the clutch and brake. The three kids not holding the brake shoveled ears of corn into the grinder until our fingers and toes were numb from the cold. We were not able to talk to each other over the roar of the machines.

Heifers and Steers

Heifers were young cows that had not yet given birth to a calf. Although they didn't need to be milked, they still had to be fed. The heifers were kept on the north end of the barn, and we brought hay from the haymow to feed them daily. A heifer has her first calf when she is two years old, after which she begins to produce milk. The two months she is not milking—before she has a calf—is called her dry period. When a male calf was born, Dad castrated it; and it became one of our steers to be fattened for market.

After we had washed and disinfected the stainless steel milkers, we were done with our chores for the day. I remember the glow of the light from the kitchen and the smell of wood smoke drifting up from the house. It was gratifying to feel that another's day work was done and we could now relax in our warm, cozy house. We did homework and played cards until bedtime.

Bringing the Cattle Home

Summer chores were more relaxed because the cows grazed in the pasture. Our evening chores began about 4:00, when we hauled grain from the granary to the mangers in a small wagon. We followed a well-worn cattle path to the pasture to bring the Holsteins home. As we went by the pond the seagulls dived at us, so we had to run. We called, "Come, Bossy!" and the cows began their trek home to milk and feed.

If a cow delivered a calf, she might swing her head toward us and bellow to protect her new baby. Certain she would charge us, we hightailed it out of there. On these occasions, Dad walked out to get the cows instead. Dad would carry the calf home, while the cow, bellowing, followed behind.

Sometimes we watched Dad deliver a calf. With the heifer lying down, we could see the two feet sticking out. Dad would tie a rope around them and pull out the calf.

The Cows Are Out

"THE COWS ARE OUT" meant we had to drop everything and help. My Dad was a reasonable man, but when it came to chasing cattle he misconstrued how we girls perceived the situation. Periodically, cows found a breach in a fence and walked out because the grass on the other side was a succulent treat for them.

"The cows are out!" Dad yelled. "Girls, stand on the north side of the gate and head them into the pasture. Warren and I will circle around in front of them and turn them down the driveway to the gate."

We knew the drill: Flail our arms in the air and holler so that the 1,000-pound Holsteins would be so scared of us three little girls they would turn back and run through the pasture gate.

Following orders, we took our places north of the gate, finding it easy to wave our arms and holler with the cattle a quarter mile away. However, as they got closer, our fear of stampeding cattle became greater than our ability to obey orders.

"Do you think they see the gate?" I asked with an ashen face, breathing in ragged gasps.

"They're going too fast to see a gate," one of my sisters replied.

"Do you think they see us?"

"I don't think they see well."

"They're stampeding straight at us!" we shouted as we hightailed it behind the barn.

As Warren and Dad tried to herd the cows toward the gate, we peeked from behind the barn and, sure enough, twenty-five cows ran right by the open gate, by the barn, and up the hill to our front lawn.

"What is WRONG with you girls?" Dad bellowed.

We whispered, "They charged us."

"Go with Warren, circle around behind them, and I will head them into the pasture."

Later, at the dinner table, Dad commented, "There is something wrong with you girls. Why is it so hard to follow orders when chasing cattle?"

Mom slammed her coffee cup on the table. "Milton, I don't blame the girls one bit. I wouldn't be foolish enough to stand there as a herd of 1,500-pound stampeding cows charged toward me."

"Whose side are you on?" asked Dad. "I guess it's easy to figure out where they get their crazy fear of cows!"

A couple days later, some cows swam across the slough on the east side of the road.

"I will scare them across the slough," Dad said as he grabbed his rifle. "Warren, move them toward home when they swim across. Girls, head them toward the cattle pass."

Daryl took the station with us girls. As Dad shot into the air to scare the cattle into swimming across the slough, Daryl screamed, "Duck! I think he's shooting at us!" He hit the ground facedown with his arms spread out. Not having time to assess the predicament, we did what any normal girls would do—we flattened ourselves to the ground, too. We found this position a rather hard one to explain to Dad.

Time after time, we knew the drill, we prepared for the chase, but something denied us the courage to remain there at the last minute. Mom said it was common sense.

Fencing

When cattle broke through the electric fences, Dad knew a weed touching the fence had grounded out the battery. He sent us kids to walk the fence line and cut any thistles that were touching the wire.

Our standard method of testing whether the electric fence worked was to pull a reed of grass and touch it to the fence. If we got a shock, it was working. Knowing that the current going through the wire was small, Dad teased us.

"I wonder if the fence is working," he said as he took a long piece of green grass and touched the fence with it. "Shucks, I don't feel a thing. Here, you try it."

Pulling a reed of grass and touching the fence, I screamed with a shock, "It's working!"

On a rainy day, Dad collected his leather gloves, pliers, posthole digger, wire cutter, and one of us kids, and then headed out to mend fences. Barbed wire fences and electric fences enclosed our fields and pastures.

Barbed wire fences consisted of three strands of barbed wire attached to wooden posts made from tree trunks. The sharp barbs on the strong wire discouraged pigs from getting through. If Dad needed to dig a new hole for a post, he used the posthole digger, which was a shovel with two handles. We unrolled the barbed wire while Dad attached it to an oak fencepost with a U-shaped wire nail called a staple. If a new hole had to be dug, Dad did it.

Farrowing Time

A few days before a sow's delivery date in the warm spring months, Dad put her in a farrowing pen. We checked on them often so we could watch them farrow. As each of the eight to twelve piglets was born, it moved to drink milk from the mother. When the sow delivered the last piglet, we ran to announce the news to Mom or Dad. Over the next few weeks, we watched the playful baby pigs fighting for nourishment. When we held them, they squealed.

Our gentle pigs loved it when we scratched them. We fed them whole ears of corn. We raised the pigs until they finished off at a certain weight and went to market.

Like Charlotte's Wilbur, our pigs scratched themselves against walls, rooted under and broke fences, ransacked their pens, chased each other in circles, squealed when scared, and grunted when satisfied and happy. A pig's natural instinct was to dig for roots. To cool off, they tipped their water troughs to create a mud puddle and laid in it. Dad said it was important to have shade for our white pigs so they would not sunburn.

Gathering Eggs

Each spring Dad would buy baby chicks from the hatchery in Dalton. They went into the brooder house where a hanging heat lamp provided warmth. We filled Mason jars with water and screwed them to saucer-like water dispensers. The chicks learned to eat finely ground corn.

We raised chickens for our family to eat, and we sold a few extra eggs. By summer, the young hens laid about one egg a day. We collected the eggs once a day, cleaned them, and put them in boxes for Mom to sell at the creamery.

Mom, Dad, and Grandma butchered and cleaned the young male chickens when they were still young and tender. They were stored in our rented freezer box in the locker plant in Dalton. In the fall, the hens were butchered. These were stewing hens that we used to make pressed chicken, a Scandinavian delicacy.

The righteous care for the needs of their animals . . .
–Proverbs 12:10 (NIV)

CHAPTER 8

Don't Pop the Clutch

Our farm was a family-run establishment that required all members of the family to contribute, and working the fields was a central part of that operation. In the spring, we planted corn, oats, and wheat. In the summer, we cultivated corn, cut and stored hay, and harvested grains; and in the fall, we harvested corn. Most crops were grown for cattle and pig feed, but extra oats or corn were sold when we needed money.

After World War II, Dad transitioned from using horses to tractors in the field. Having two tractors, Dad and Warren plowed, harrowed, planted, cultivated, mowed, and combined, while we girls assisted with picking rock, hauling hay and straw, and unloading grain. Most of the work we girls did was a group effort—rarely did we work on our own. While Dad and Warren spent long days driving the tractors back and forth across the fields, we girls completed the barn chores, except for milking.

In fall, after the harvest, Dad and Warren plowed under the stubble, preparing the fields for the following spring. During the winter months, Dad and Warren spread manure from the barn on the fields for fertilizer. In spring, when the fields dried, Dad and Warren broke up the big clods until the field developed into a fine consistency for planting.

Driving the Allis-Chalmers Tractor

We girls took turns driving the 1949 Allis-Chalmers for picking rock and hauling hay. Dad used a crank to start it for us. Driving the orange tricycle-shaped tractor was exciting, even though working the clutch presented a challenge. "Let the clutch out gently—don't pop it," Dad warned us. After Dad set the throttle, we started the tractor in motion by letting out the clutch gently so it wouldn't lurch. When Dad hollered, "Stop the tractor," we pushed in the clutch and brake pedals at the same time.

Dad was a good boss. If we made a mistake, he did not holler at us. He would just shake his head and walk away, making us feel disappointed and wanting to try harder. I think he didn't holler because he wished we didn't have to do all this work.

Rock Picking

Every spring, we missed school for two days so we could pick rocks. The farm machinery brought some rocks to the surface, but it was mainly weather and erosion that forced rocks and stones to emerge each year. Each spring we asked Dad about these rocks. He said we should read about the effect that glaciers had on the soil.

We girls took turns driving the tractor steadily over the fields, pulling a stone boat. When we were not driving the tractor, we picked rocks and placed them on the stone boat. When the stone boat was full, we emptied it by pitching the rocks into a pile along our property lines.

Dad's humor and conversations made these days enjoyable. He explained how drought, hail, and wind damage could affect our livelihood and told us about the importance of how many bushels to the acre and the price of wheat. We discussed why we identified Minnesota as the North Star State, how pheasants came to Minnesota from Europe, and why weather was crucial to farming. We learned a lot from Dad and enjoyed spending this time with him.

Harvesting Hay

The first harvest happened in early June, when the alfalfa bloomed in purple flowers. Three times a summer, Dad and Warren mowed the alfalfa using a sickle-bar mower, raked it into swaths, and let it dry for a day. As Dad ran the tractor-pulled round baler over the long windrows, it gathered the alfalfa, baled it, and tied it with binder twine. Finally, fifty-pound round bales popped out. This baler was the one piece of farm equipment that gave Dad the most trouble. If it got clogged or if the twine broke, Dad had to stop and repair it before he could go on.

The following day, we girls, wearing long pants and long-sleeved cotton shirts to prevent the prickly hay from scratching our skin, assisted with hauling the hay bales to the haymow. Because driving the tractor was easier work than handling the bales, Dad insisted we girls rotate this job. One girl drove the tractor, which pulled the hayrack, while Warren and two girls walked along, lifted the bales by hand using two hay hooks, and threw them onto the hayrack where Dad stacked them securely.

Once the hayrack was bursting with a full load, Dad drove to the barn with us kids sitting on top of the hay bales, enjoying our ride on the hayrack as it moved and swayed over rolling ground and through ditches, seeming at times to almost tip.

At the barn, Dad put the bales on the elevator, which carried them to a ceiling-mounted hay carrier track near the rafters in the center of the huge haymow. In the hot hayloft, one of us kids guided each bale from the elevator onto a bale-carrier track mounted on the hayloft's ceiling. When the bale pile got so high that the bales could not move, we kids stood on top of it, near the ceiling of the hayloft, and pushed bales off the moving carrier. The faster Dad put bales on the elevator, the faster we worked. Working in the hayloft was a hot, sweaty job. These were the days I really appreciated the ice-cold water from the hose in the milk room.

We enjoyed working with Dad because of his humor and laughter. "It's a real scorcher out here today, so we better go swimming after chores," Dad said to motivate us. Years later, I realized his real motive was getting us to wash away the layers of dirt that had accumulated on our bodies.

Golden Fields of Wheat, Oats, and Barley

Dad planted grains by pulling a fourteen-foot drill behind the tractor. The drill had disks that created shallow trenches in the soil and then dropped seeds from a seed box into these trenches. Chains dragged behind the drill, covering the trenches.

When the wheat ripened, it was harvested immediately, before rain, hail, or a tornado could ravage it. In July and August, Dad and Warren swatted the golden fields of oats and wheat into windrows. Dad drove the tractor with a pull-type combine behind, separating the grain from the shaft, which was later raked and baled for straw.

One hot and muggy July afternoon, time was of utmost importance because it looked like rain. When the hopper was full, Dad stopped the tractor, which was Warren's signal to drive the box wagon under the grain hopper so Dad could unload the hopper. A half-mile away, Warren knew to jump into action the minute the combine stopped. However, on this particular afternoon Warren was engrossed in a novel while waiting for his signal. Dad hollered and waved, but Warren did not hear or see anything other than words on a page. Finally, Dad, tired of hollering, walked across the field to get Warren, who glanced up to see Dad five feet away. Warren's punishment was losing his reading privileges, although Dad reneged on that threat after a few hours because he needed Warren's assistance as much as Warren needed his books.

When the grain wagon was full, Warren drove it to the granary where we girls helped to unload it. We crawled into the wagon, full of grain and itchy dust, and shoveled the grain toward an auger, which carried it to a bin in the granary. I disliked this job and, to make matters worse, Audrey developed a rash from the dusty grain, so she was allowed to do housework while Jo and I shoveled the grain.

Sometimes Warren drove the tractor to the grain elevator in Dalton, where there were lines of farmers waiting to dump their grain. The grain elevator was located by the railroad tracks since grain was transported by rail. Although Warren was not old enough to drive on public roads, nobody ever said anything because they understood it was important for farming.

With the grain fields harvested, Dad and Warren raked the shaft into rows. Dad ran the tractor-pulled baler over the long windrows, which lifted the straw, tied it with binder twine, and pushed out straw bales. We girls helped Dad and Warren haul the straw bales home and stack them in the hayloft. When winter came, we pitched these bales down for bedding for the livestock.

Wheat Comes First

It was vital to harvest the wheat at the right time, before hail or a strong wind flattened the field. In fact, it was so important that it took precedence over everything else. When Mom went into labor with her eighth child, Dad had no choice but to drop off Mom at the Fergus Falls Hospital and return to harvesting wheat. I was in the kitchen, preparing meals and taking care of my younger siblings, when the phone call came telling us we had a new sister and that I should run to the field and give the news to Dad. He was excited, of course, but he had to continue with the harvesting rather than stop to go see his newest child.

Corn Harvest

Dad planted the cornrows himself because he wanted them to be straight, which required experience. In the absence of weed killers, Warren cultivated each cornfield three times. He said it was an awful job because we always had to stare down the straight rows so as not to veer off course and cultivate the corn instead of the weeds. It was important to focus and not get distracted. Warren said it was boring work, and he had to spend most of the month of June doing it.

After the first frost, Dad harvested the corn with a two-row corn picker. Each wagonload of corn was delivered to the farmyard and put into a corncrib. During the winter months, we ground the corn into feed for the livestock. If it was an exceptionally rainy fall, the corn was not picked until the ground froze. Some of the corn became silage by chopping the corn and the stalk and blowing it into the silo.

Although field work could be challenging, it gave us a sense of accomplishment, knowing that we each had a part to play in keeping the family farm running. When the day was over, we were tired, but it was a good kind of tired.

They sowed fields and planted vineyards that yielded a fruitful harvest.
–Psalm 107:37 (NIV)

Sunday Dinner

CHAPTER 9

Cooking and Baking from Scratch

We girls enjoyed cooking and baking. Whereas cleaning felt like monotonous drudgery, we threw ourselves enthusiastically into preparing food. When we first baked, we worked side by side with Mom, learning the skills. Eventually, however, Mom gave us complete autonomy in preparing meals and baking while she spent time alone in the garden or was busy with babies, mending, cleaning, running errands for Dad, or doing one of a million other chores. By letting us take charge in the kitchen, Mom taught us girls leadership. She also trained us to step out and take a risk when we were not quite sure what to do.

We had permission to be creative in the kitchen. We tried new things and made lots of mistakes, but Mom and Dad never squashed our ideas with criticism. Mom made sure we felt a sense of self-worth by lavishing us with praise in front of family and friends.

The Cast-Iron Stove

We cooked on a wood-burning cast-iron cookstove with a four-lid cooking surface. To get the fire going, we placed a lid-lifter into a groove on the round plates then put small strips of kindling and crumpled newspaper inside the firebox. After the kindling was burning well, we added larger pieces of wood and used a poker to stir the fire. We learned to shake the grates so old ashes would drop into an ash pan, and we adjusted the damper in the stovepipe to allow smoke to go up the chimney.

We fried lefse on top of the cast-iron stove. Mom and Grandma were hesitant to replace the wood-burning range with a gas range until they were able to purchase a lefse griddle, which they eventually did at which time we got a new gas stove.

A Lump of Butter and Flour to Thicken

We girls baked every day when we were not in school—cookies, cakes, bars, and pies. Unlimited supplies of eggs, butter, lard, sugar, flour, milk, and cream (skimmed fresh off the milk in the barn), as well as rhubarb, apples, chokecherries, and strawberries were available to us. Spices, sugar, cocoa, and shortening filled the pantry shelves, and a flour bin held a fifty-pound sack of flour. Lard came in silver metal lard pails from the locker plant.

We searched Mom's recipe box (the Norwegian recipes my mother had gotten from Grandma Galena), the *Our Saviors Lutheran Church Cookbook*, *The Betty Crocker Cookbook*, and magazines for new recipes. Many of Mom's recipes only listed ingredients but not amounts or baking times. Mom (and the women before her) had made these recipes so often, they knew how to put everything together and for how long—they didn't need to have it written down.

We girls learned to cook through a process of hollering questions to Mom, who was in a different room or in the garden.

"Mom, how much is a pinch?" I yelled while reading a handwritten recipe card.

"Just a smidgen," she answered from the dining room as she sewed patches on jeans.

"How much is a smidgen?"

"Just a little bit—whatever you think."

"Mom, how much is a lump of butter?"

She ignored me, so I guessed.

Filling our tin flour sifter, I pinched the handle several times and shook it side to side until flour fell into the bowl.

"Mom, how much is 'flour to thicken'?"

"Just enough so the dough isn't too sticky to roll into balls," she answered.

Making peanut butter cookies, I beat eggs with a hand-operated rotary eggbeater. Jo stood at the counter, rolling the dough into balls.

"Mom, it says to press with a fork. What does that mean?"

"It means to press with a fork." Apparently, sometimes Mom grew tired of our questions.

We used a coffee cup to measure Spry shortening and used silverware as measuring spoons for soda, salt, and spices. I learned to calculate how many tablespoons are in a cup and how many ounces are in a pint, to add a "dab" of vinegar or lemon juice to milk to make it sour, and to test for doneness by sticking a straw from the kitchen broom into the center of a cake.

"It says to beat the frosting for a while. How long is a while?"

"Beat it for 350 strokes and not one less."

I cut the lard into the flour, rolled out two flaky piecrusts, crimped the edges with a fork, poked holes in the crust, and placed it in the hot oven, remembering the rule of not handling the piecrust more than I had to. After rolling and squeezing a lemon to get juice, I scraped it on a shredder to get pieces of rind. I separated eggs, saving the whites for the meringue on the lemon pie.

I made every variety of cream pie in *The Betty Crocker Cookbook*: banana cream, butterscotch cream, coconut cream, and pineapple cream. However, everyone's favorite pies were rhubarb, apple, and lemon. Home-canned apples, cherries, peaches, blackberries, rhubarb, blueberries, and strawberries provided most of the fruit for winter pies. Custard or pudding was made from farm milk and eggs.

Home-baked Bread and Rolls

Bread was a major food staple in our home, and Mom baked it twice a week. Bread and butter were served with every meal, and it was what we kids ate when we got home from school each day before beginning our chores. Unfortunately, as a youngster, I never appreciated homemade bread as much as I did the jam, honey, or brown sugar we spread on it.

Making good bread was an art that Mom did not share with us girls. She mixed the bread dough the evening before it was to be baked. When the square little compressed yeast cakes had dissolved in warm water, she mixed them with flour in a large round aluminum dishpan and added scalded milk. I remember her beating this mixture until it formed a ball. She covered the pan with a dishtowel and set the dough to rise all night.

The next morning she kneaded it, sometimes adding a little more flour. Then she shaped it into buns or loaves and let it rise again. About noon, the first pan was baked. As the last pan of buns came out of the oven, we ate them with brown sugar.

Meals and Lunches

Happy to relinquish the responsibility of preparing meals, Mom preferred gardening or mending. While we girls were allowed to be creative with baking, meals were expected to consist of the hearty meat and potatoes that Dad favored. We did not need recipes to prepare these meals—we knew them by heart. Meat was fried in a skillet or roasted in the oven, while vegetables were boiled. Meat and vegetable dishes were seasoned with salt, pepper, onion, and lots of butter.

We grew most of our own vegetables. In the summer, they were picked fresh daily from the garden, and for the rest of the year they came from our supply of canned vegetables in the cellar. We savored the bounty from our garden—we would dig potatoes or carrots, pick peas or string beans, or cut a head of fresh cabbage to eat with a meal. The cabbage was boiled in lightly salted water and drained; then we added heavy cream, thickened it with flour, and seasoned it with a slab of butter. For canned corn and green beans, we heated them in the liquid they were canned in, then drained and served them with a slab of butter. Mom's favorite June meal was creamed fresh peas and new potatoes.

We obtained meat, milk, cream, eggs, and butter from our animals. When our supply of pork or beef ran low, Dad hauled a steer or hog to the locker plant in Dalton, where they slaughtered it, butchered it, wrapped family-size portions in white butcher paper, and stamped the wrapping in blue ink to identify the contents. The meat was frozen and stored in a locker box that we rented. Every day Dad brought some meat home from the locker plant.

Dad ate pickled herring, liver, blood sausage, fish balls, oysters, lutefisk, venison, duck, and pheasant. Although Mom prepared these for Dad, she refused to eat these "disgusting" victuals, so we girls decided not to eat them either.

Breakfast

Breakfast was the first meal of the day, as soon as we got up. Mom and we kids ate cereal, oatmeal, or bread and jam. Mom fried eggs and ham or bacon for Dad. We drank water with most of our meals. I was not fond of raw milk, but I liked thick cream on cereal. Of course, adults drank coffee all day long, but kids did not drink it until they graduated from high school.

Dinner

We had our main dinner at noon, except on school days when we had it in the evenings. Dinner was the standard fare of meat, potatoes, gravy, vegetables, bread, and a dessert of fruit sauce, pie, or pudding. Using two heavy cast-iron skillets, we fried pork chops, steak, and meatballs in melted lard, adding chopped onions, salt, and pepper. Steak was rolled in flour before being fried. When the meat was done, we made pan-fried gravy by draining the potato water into the skillet drippings then adding a mixture of flour and water. If we had pork chops, we made milk gravy.

Timing was perhaps the greatest lesson we learned. We set the table (with the salt, pepper, and butter dish in the middle), sliced the bread, drained the potato water into the skillet to make gravy, and added the flour and water. I remember scorching the potatoes many times.

Leftovers for Supper

Supper, at the end of the day, was a lighter meal. It frequently consisted of meats that had been prepared earlier served with vegetables, fried potatoes, home-baked bread, or soup. We used leftovers from dinner, simmering roast beef and potatoes in heavy cream for hash, making hot beef sandwiches with a big mound of mashed potatoes, or frying up ham or hamburgers and leftover potatoes.

In summer, we savored sweet corn and strawberries with cream. Corn on the cob alone made a complete evening supper for us kids. Dad planted a couple rows of sweet corn seed at the edge of the cornfield, but we often ate field corn if it was still full of its milky juice.

On Fridays, our no-meat day, we often had pancakes for supper with homemade syrup. To make the syrup, we boiled water and brown sugar and added drops of maple flavoring that Mom had purchased from the Watkins man.

Mealtime

Mealtimes conjure warm, pleasant memories for me. Our family sat for dinner and supper together at the large kitchen table. Everyone had their own place, with Mom and Dad at either end of the table. Mom was the last one to sit, and no one began eating until she was seated. We had lively conversations while we ate, bantering and discussing a variety of topics. Mealtime was our time to be heard.

Sunday Meals

Mom cooked on Sunday, and we assembled for a formal meal in our dining room, using a white linen tablecloth with our best china and silverware. Pickles and a lime Jell-O with shredded carrots and cabbage salad were added to the menu to make the Sunday meal special. This was the only day of the week we had mashed potatoes, which was everyone's favorite.

Mom cut a chicken, rolled it in flour and spices, and fried it in hot lard before baking it in the oven along with scalloped corn. When it was time to eat, she added cream to the drippings to make gravy, while we girls mashed the potatoes with a hand-held potato masher and prepared a jar of canned vegetables. This meal ended with a homemade pie I had made. On Sunday evenings we ate barbecue on Mom's homemade buns, along with a rice salad.

Midmorning Coffee and Afternoon Lunch

Lunch was the term used for sandwiches, cookies, with coffee or water, eaten between breakfast and dinner, or between dinner and supper. Physical labor on the farm burned up many calories, so lunch provided energy and a bit of rest from a long day's work. During threshing, we kids took lunches and water out to the field in both midmorning and the afternoon. Along with sandwiches and cake or cookies, we often brought hot coffee in Mason jars, wrapped in newspaper and a dishtowel, to Warren and Dad, who were working in the field.

Any time a visitor stopped by, they were offered coffee and cookies—our green gallon cookie jar was always full of cookies. Lunch was the word we used to describe serving refreshments to afternoon or evening visitors at home, as well as providing a piece of cake or cookies after special school or church events. Before visitors went home at midnight, lunch was served.

Doing the Dishes

Doing the dishes was an inevitable routine three times a day for us three older girls, so we rotated washing, drying, and clearing. The "person washing" filled a dishpan with hot soapy water and washed the glasses and silverware, then the Melmac plates, and finally the black cast iron fry pans and hard-to-clean pots and pans. After rinsing the dishes in scalding water and placing them in a dish drainer, the "person drying" wiped them dry with several flour-sack dishtowels and put them away. The "person clearing" brought in the dishes from the table and piled them next to the sink, carried the slop bucket to the pigs, fed leftover scraps to our dog Rex, emptied a grease can used for meat drippings, burned paper in the burn barrel in the woods, and swept the kitchen floor. While we worked, we discussed a multitude of topics.

Reflections

Food—especially ethnic food—was an important aspect of hospitality. Card parties, afternoon sewing bees, Ladies Aid meetings, short visits, unplanned visits, holidays, Halloween parties, neighborhood visits, Sunday afternoon visits, Friday night visits, 4-H meetings—every get-together somehow involved food.

We did not have a blender, electric mixer, deep freeze, microwave, electric stove, dishwasher, or garbage disposal. We mashed potatoes and whipped cream by hand, and we never used margarine. (Dad believed that butter sales were critical for dairy farmers' success, so he despised oleomargarine.) We did not use mixes, get carryout, or eat fast food—nearly everything was made from scratch.

We girls developed into respectable cooks, but looking back I realize we thought we were better cooks than we actually were. We knew how to flavor things well with salt, pepper, and onions. We boiled and creamed vegetables but did not blanch, braise, or steam them. We had not even heard of those terms. We fried steaks, hamburgers, pork chops, and bacon but we did not sauté or stir-fry; and we roasted meat in an oven but did not grill, broil, or barbeque. I never saw an outdoor barbeque grill until I moved out of the Dalton community.

Nothing was wasted. The discarded potato peels and other food scraps were fed to the pigs. When a pig was butchered, we rendered the lard (processed fat) to use for frying, and we also used the intestines, boiled the head, and pickled the feet.

Growing up, we did not eat sauerkraut, seafood, pizza, spaghetti, or even "hotdish" at home. Our food options were limited, but we didn't know any other way at the time.

A person can do nothing better than
to eat and drink and find satisfaction in their own toil.
This too, I see, is from the hand of God.
–Ecclesiastes 2:24 (NIV)

CHAPTER 10

Garden Produce and a Blue Speckled Canner

There were few things more satisfying to Mom than working in the vegetable garden and preserving food. She said she liked the sound of the garden silence; she could hear herself think there. While she enjoyed the solitude of laboring with her fruits and vegetables, we girls loved that her time in the garden gave us autonomy in the kitchen. It was Mom's garden—she planted, weeded, and harvested it, and it provided our family with fresh produce for the summer months and canned fruits and vegetables for the remainder of the year. Mom had no choice but to have a large garden because she had such a large family to feed.

Planted in full sunlight, the garden site was a large plot of land at the end of the field east of the house, an easy location to visit frequently. Dad prepared the soil for Mom's garden every spring, and they used manure for fertilizer. All seeds were sown directly into the dirt. I do not remember Mom watering the garden. If she did, it had to be by hauling buckets of water because we did not own a hose.

Planting, Weeding, and Hoeing

As soon as the black earth dried, Dad plowed, disked, and harrowed Mom's large garden patch. Before Memorial Day, Mom planted potatoes, carrots, cucumbers, cabbage, beets, string beans, peas, tomatoes, squash, rutabagas, onions, dill, radishes, and melons. Putting sticks at each end of the garden, she strung twine between them to assure her rows were straight. To plant, she pulled a furrow with a hoe adjacent to the twine, set in the seeds, covered them with the hoe, and tamped the soil down with her foot. She attached the empty seed packet to the stick at the end of each row. After the plants emerged, she thinned the seedlings to allow growth for the strongest plants. As the hot summer wore on, most mornings she hoed weeds from the garden.

Rhubarb

Rhubarb was the first crop ready. We made rhubarb sauce, rhubarb jam, rhubarb crisp, rhubarb pie, and rhubarb bars. Mom canned quarts of rhubarb sauce for winter dessert, and we froze rhubarb for winter pies—one of our favorites. I made more than thirty rhubarb pies a year. Mom said the harvest season for rhubarb lasted until the middle of July, and after that the stalks were too woody to be good.

The Strawberry Patch

In the spring, Mom removed the straw that had been a

winter jacket on her strawberry plants. Mom's strawberry patch produced hundreds of quarts of big juicy strawberries for fresh eating, freezing, jam, pies, cakes, and other desserts. When people wanted to know what her secret to such a bountiful strawberry production was, she told them it was lots of sun and the good cow manure Dad spread on the patch each spring.

We ate fresh strawberries covered with sugar and heavy cream, strawberry shortcake, strawberry sauce, and strawberry jam. When friends or relatives came to visit in the summertime, they were pressed to take home fresh strawberries, rhubarb, or sweet corn.

Sweet Corn

Using the corn planter, Dad planted a few rows of sweet corn along the edge of a cornfield. When the kernels in the center of the ears were full and "milky," the corn was picked and husked immediately before the supper meal. Back in the house, it was placed in a large pot of boiling water for five minutes. Steaming corn on the cob, served on a big platter with butter, salt, and pepper, was a complete meal and one of our favorites.

Chokecherries

The last week in July, Mom dispatched us kids with metal buckets to the far side of the farm to pick clusters of purple chokecherries. The chokecherry grows as a large shrub or small tree with sharply toothed leaves. Its fruits are like small cherries, red at first, turning purple to black at maturity.

Returning home, we stemmed and cleaned the chokecherries. Mom covered them with water and boiled them, drained the juice, covered them with water again, and boiled them a second time.

Draining the berries, Mom mixed the two juices together, brought this new mixture to a boil, added three cups of water, covered it, and let it simmer for fifteen minutes before running the sweet-smelling juice through a cotton towel and then canning it in quart jars.

When we wanted to make jelly, we followed the directions on the Sure-Jell package. I remember it being something like boiling the chokecherry juice, sugar, and Sure-Jell for about three minutes. I thought hot chokecherry jelly on fresh homemade bread was a small piece of heaven on earth. Neighbors and relatives who dropped in for a visit during chokecherry season received a jar of Mom's canned chokecherry juice.

Big Yellow Apples

I have yet to find a tree with apples as delicious and bountiful as they were on our backyard apple tree. These were yellow tart pie apples. With a greenish-yellow color, the apples were ready to be picked in late August. We were careful to avoid the apples with punctures or bruises, but because these apples were so good, we picked every one we could, even those that had fallen to the ground. We gave away what we did not use to make applesauce, pie filling, and apple crisp.

I made hundreds of apple pies. First I made the piecrusts; then I peeled and cut the apples, added sugar, a dash of cinnamon, a little flour, and mixed it all together. (I ate about ten pieces of apple myself, so I always prepared extra.) I poured the apples into the bottom crust and added the top crust, fluted the edges, cut slits on top, and sprinkled sugar to top it off. When we made apples pies, we always made two or three. Our apple pies had a nice brown filling since we did not put lemon juice on the apples to keep them from browning. We preferred it this way.

I have never had applesauce as good as what Mom made.

I think the secret to Mom's applesauce was that she made it chunky by not pressing it through a sieve, and she added a cinnamon stick or two to each jar before sealing.

Locker Plant

Like most people, we did not have a freezer, so we rented huge drawers in Dalton's walk-in locker plant. Besides keeping beef, chicken, and pork in this freezer, we prepared and froze delicious yellow pie apples, rhubarb, strawberries, and corn to store in this drawer. We peeled and cored the apples, cut them into slices, and sealed them in plastic bags before sending them to the locker plant.

Dad stopped at our locker, which was located adjacent to the creamery, every day to get meat. I hurried whenever I had to get items from our locker drawer in this windowless, zero-degree freezer room, concerned that the door might lock on me.

Canning

Although gardening was the first step, canning was equally important, and for this Mom needed us girls to help. Mom canned hundreds of quarts and pints of fruits and vegetables each year. She saw canning fruits and vegetable as an artistic endeavor, and at summer's end her art pieces lined wooden shelves along the cellar wall and provided our family with fruit and vegetables for an entire year. The vegetables, strawberries, chokecherries, apples, and rhubarb grew on our farm; but the peaches, cherries, and pears that we canned came in wooden bins from the general store. Sauce, which was served as a dessert, is what we called home-canned peaches, pears, apples, rhubarb, and cherries.

I imagine every mother-and-daughter team in the 1950s

canned fruits and vegetables together. After spending twelve or thirteen years assisting Mom, I was confidently able to complete the steps in the process myself. Mom loved this activity, and we girls found it enjoyable, too.

Since we used the same Kerr and Ball jars and rings from year to year, we sterilized them to prevent botulism. We used new rubber seals each year, also sterilizing them in boiling water. Mom hauled out her blue-speckled canner with a wire rack inside, which processed seven quarts at a time.

I scalded the peaches to loosen the skins before peeling them. Immediately after removing a peach from the boiling water, I plunged it into cold water for a second to make it easier to handle while removing the skin, and then I cut it in half and removed the pit. Like a game of hot potato, I scalded my hand on each fuzzy peach.

While we girls immersed peaches and slipped off the skins, Mom packed them in quart jars, poured in boiling sugar-water syrup to half an inch from the top, covered the jars with new seals and the previous year's screw-on rims, and partially tightened the covers, leaving room for expansion. Not having a pressure cooker, Mom placed the jars in the large blue canner to boil. After the sterilizing process, she tightened the covers and placed them upside-down on a dishtowel on the counter, allowing them to cool.

We repeated a similar process on another day for cherries, rhubarb, pears, and applesauce. I pared, cored, and quartered big yellow pie apples, cleaned and cut rhubarb into one-inch pieces, and stemmed cherries. When we harvested the vegetables, I removed the shucks and silks before slicing corn off the cob, snapped green beans, and shelled peas.

Late Fall Harvest

When an early fall night felt as if there might be a frost, Mama sent us girls out to cover the garden with old sheets to protect what was still growing. In the morning, we uncovered the plants for another day of growth in the warm sun. Often there might be a frost followed by several more weeks of mild weather. The green tomatoes remaining in the garden were brought inside to ripen on windowsills.

We girls helped harvest the potatoes and place them in gunnysacks. Potatoes and carrots were stored in the cellar for winter use, along with hundreds of glass quart jars of home-canned produce. Thanks to Mom's amazing gardening and canning skills, we were able to eat delicious fruits and vegetables year-round.

Then God said, "I give you every seed-bearing plant on the face
of the whole earth and every tree that has fruit with seed in it.
They will be yours for food."
–Genesis 1:29 (NIV)

Our First Dryer

CHAPTER 11

The Wringer Washer

One of the primary advances since my childhood is how we spend our time. Today, I can read a book, run to the store, or watch a movie while my clothes are washing and drying. During my childhood, undertaking the chore of washing clothes for a family of ten was a time-consuming activity that occupied most of a day.

When not in school, we girls managed the wash (we did not use the word laundry). Monday was the day designated for this chore. In wintertime, we wheeled the wringer washing machine into the kitchen. In summer we left it on the porch. Our first task was to sort the clothes into piles, followed by soaking the white socks and dishtowels in bleach in the kitchen sink. Using the same water for every load, we washed whites first and then lights, then darks, and finally barn clothing.

In summertime, we draped the washed clothes on five long clotheslines strung between two sturdy wooden posts. With the sun hitting my shoulders and wind blowing my hair, I grabbed a wood clothespin from the hanging clothespin bags and then hung things together by color and size, connecting towels and diapers to ration clothespins. Like other families in our community, we followed the rules of modesty on the clothesline. We pinned underwear on the back line behind sheets or towels, out of sight of visitors. In the winter, we let the clothes freeze dry on the line and then brought them in to thaw and dry on clothes racks in the kitchen.

To empty the washing machine tub, I detached a hose from a short hook fastened to the side and lowered it, catching the water in a bucket to haul outside for watering flowers. I cleaned the agitator and rolled the machine to the porch where it remained until the next Monday.

Folding and Ironing

Once the clothes were dry, we girls carried them in, folded diapers and towels, sorted socks, underwear, and undershirts for each family member, and assembled sheets on beds using Mom's Army-inspired tuck-under regime. Diapers were folded in thirds and then in half and in half again. We rolled pairs of socks in balls, folding one sock over the other, and put them in an empty shoebox in a drawer. We folded bath towels, hand towels, and washcloths.

We ironed hand-embroidered dishtowels, tablecloths, pillowcases, aprons, shirts, slacks, and jeans. Lacking a steam iron, we sprinkled the clothes with water before ironing them. Grandma used a metal stopper with holes in it that she put on top of an empty pop bottle, but we just dipped our hand in water and shook it on each piece of clothing before rolling it. As we pressed the damp fabric with a hot iron, the dampness was absorbed and the wrinkles came out.

An electric clothes dryer was one of the first major household purchases our family made. It came after the fifth child was born and five years before a bathroom was added. There just was not enough room in the kitchen to dry clothes for seven people. We did not use the dryer in summer because that would have been a wasteful use of electricity.

> *But as for you, be strong and do not give up,*
> *for your work will be rewarded.*
> 2 Chronicles 15:7 (NIV)

CHAPTER 12

Cleanliness Is Next to Godliness

Cleanliness is next to godliness—that is what my mother believed, and she disliked having a caller find her house in any state of disarray. An orderly and disciplined housekeeper, Mom established routines and schedules for us girls to follow. Daily, we made the beds, dusted and dust-mopped all the floors, shook the rugs outside, did the dishes, babysat the toddlers, and burned garbage in the burn barrel. Weekly, we sanitized the outhouse, scrubbed and waxed the kitchen floor, and dusted furniture. When needed, we polished silver, defrosted the refrigerator freezer, shined shoes, and mowed the grass. Whereas I enjoyed cooking and washing clothes, I found cleaning to be drudgery.

Making the Beds

After finishing our barn chores, we made the beds and straightened up the upstairs. Mom lauded the importance of making a bed correctly so family members could peel the covers back at night and snuggle in for a sound sleep. We knew the routine: tuck in the corners of the bottom sheet in Army style (we didn't have fitted sheets), tuck any excess of the top sheet under the mattress at the foot of the bed, add blankets, smooth the chenille bedspread, plump the pillows, toss pajama bags on top of the pillows, put dirty clothes behind the bedroom doors, and store toys in their proper place.

"What are you girls doing?" Mom hollered up the stairs. "I don't hear any movement."

"We're making perfect Army corners like you taught us," we yelled back.

"Well, turn off the lights up there. Do you think we're made of money?"

Cloth Diapers

When you are the oldest girl and have six younger brothers and sisters, you quickly learn to change a diaper. Until I left for college, there was always a baby or toddler in diapers. Cloth diapers are labor intensive. They had to be rinsed, soaked, boiled, hung on the line to dry, and folded. This chore definitely fell under the "daily" category.

The white cotton flannel rectangular diapers were held in place with two plastic-headed steel safety pins. These bulky diapers came in one size; and if the baby was little, we folded the cloth four times instead of three. Rubber pull-on pants went over the cloth diapers to provide protection against leaks. Preventing diaper rash was always our number-one goal, and cornstarch was an excellent baby powder. Of course, Mom was very motivated to get the youngest child potty trained before the next baby came.

Weekly Chores

We mopped the kitchen floor at least twice a week because everyone was always "tracking in." Mom said the best way to get in the corners was on our hands and knees. When the floor dried, we used Simonize wax from a metal can to make it shiny. All the floor coverings were linoleum or wood, so a dust mop, broom, and dustpan were all we needed to get the job done.

Spring Cleaning

In the spring we opened the windows to air out the house. Then we scoured, dusted, mopped, and polished every possible thing we could clean. We scrubbed walls and baseboards; washed, starched, and stretched the sheer curtains; cleaned light fixtures; and oiled the mopboard and woodwork. We flipped mattresses, washed the chenille bedspreads, and stored the heavy winter bedding. Twice a year, the blankets spent a day airing out on the line.

We lined our dresser drawers with fresh newspapers before filling them with seasonal clothing we retrieved from the attic. In the kitchen, Mom lined the kitchen shelves with new contact paper.

Spring Yard Cleanup

After we finished the inside cleaning, we started on the yard. Everyone helped. Dad hauled away the straw banking around the house and took off the tarpaper. Dad and Mom replaced storm windows and doors with screens so we could open our windows at night and feel the fresh air. Working with the wind, we kids raked the lawn and picked up items that had been left around the yard during winter.

During the summer, we cut the grass (we never called it "mowing the lawn") with a gasoline push-mower. Then we went to Grandma's house to cut hers, too.

Battening Down for Winter

In the fall, the cycle continued as Mom washed the storm windows before helping Dad install them. Once again, Dad banked the house with straw bales, while we girls helped Mom put three or four quilts on each bed in the unheated upstairs, closed off the east rooms, set up the portable toilet in the attic, and retrieved the winter clothes, mittens, boots, and scarves from the attic. Finally, Dad took our ice skates to town to be sharpened.

If we ever complained, Mom had a favorite phrase: "If I've told you once, I've told you a hundred times: We don't have bankers' hours around here."

"Work with enthusiasm, as though you were working for the Lord rather than for people."
–Ephesians 6:7 (NIV)

CHAPTER 13

Allowance

The importance of our weekly allowance cannot be overstated. Each Saturday evening, Dad paid us each a wage of fifty cents, seventy-five cents, or one dollar, depending on our age. Because of the work we did and the rewards we received, we kids maintained an extraordinary work ethic, esteemed a job done well, appreciated the intrinsic reward of praise, and accepted our salary in the same spirit that Dad received his creamery check, since we had justifiably earned it. Our allowance was not dependent upon the chores we did, because we didn't have a choice whether or not to work—everyone in our family was required to contribute. Likewise, a punishment was never the withholding of allowance. Immersed in adult-like work from an early age, we were integral to the farm's upkeep and success. As such, we felt valued and not disadvantaged.

We prized the dollar we received each week, and it allowed us to be self-reliant. We learned how to budget a small amount of money and to save for the future. Our allowance gave us funds to spend on candy or gifts, or to save. A portion went in our church envelope, we spent a portion on ourselves, and the remainder we set aside to purchase Christmas and birthday presents. With a nickel, we could buy a bag of penny candy or an ice cream cone. If we needed extra cash, we worked out a business deal with a sibling, but we never asked our parents for money.

Impeccable Integrity

Dad was a man of impeccable integrity and honesty. He believed in telling the truth and doing the right thing and that was his greatest expectation of us kids. One night while babysitting for a neighbor, I received a five-dollar bill, when the going rate was only twenty-five cents an hour. Not happy that I had accepted charity, Dad drove me to the neighbor's house to return the bill. I explained that I must receive a fair sum.

Norwegian values taught us that to ask for money, to accept more than an honest price, or to accept welfare exemplified charity. We were expected to act independently and not rely on others to provide for us.

Mail Orders

The back of cereal boxes offered enticing prizes that could be ordered with a few box tops and a little cash. We could purchase a miniature telescope, a magnifying glass, a sundial watch, a camera, a first aid kit, a baseball bat–shaped pencil, or a Lone Ranger deputy badge.

Warren sent for a plastic submarine that would dive underwater and resurface on its own. On its bottom was a tiny container for baking powder. Another time he sent in for an official Tony the Tiger autographed baseball.

I used my money to order a set of fifty colorful bird pictures advertised on the back of a cereal box. I hung them in my bedroom, planning to date each picture when I observed the bird on our farm. One day, one of the little kids scribbled on my prized pictures. As I complained to Mom, Warren said, "It doesn't matter, Mom. It is impossible to spot all those birds in Minnesota. Do you think she will see a penguin or a roadrunner on our farm?"

To end the matter, Mom said Warren should mind his own business, and I should keep pictures out of a toddler's reach.

Club Meetings

We siblings held official club meetings for the sole purpose of combining our money to buy Christmas gifts for Mom and Dad. One of us called the meeting to order, one read the secretary's report, one read the treasurer's report, and someone else brought the treats. We held these meetings on Wednesday evenings when Mom and Dad were bowling and I was babysitting the little ones.

Savings Passbook

At the First State Bank in Dalton, each of us kids had a savings account on which we earned interest. The blue savings passbook recorded each deposit and the interest earned. The main deposit was when we sold our 4-H pigs at the county fair. That money was to go toward our college educations.

Do not store up for yourselves treasures on earth,
where moths and vermin destroy,
and where thieves break in and steal.
But store up for yourselves treasures in heaven,
where moths and vermin do not destroy,
and where thieves do not break in and steal.
For where your treasure is,
there your heart will be also.
−Matthew 6:19–21 (NIV)

PART FOUR

Play

Swimming

CHAPTER 14

Put an Egg in Your Shoe and Beat It

Work took precedence over play, but our parents were mindful of carving out sufficient time for us kids to relax and have fun. While summer mornings were for work, summer afternoons often afforded us free time to play. Many of my happiest moments from childhood came during these leisure times, which didn't require any money or the attention of our parents.

"Put an egg in your shoe and beat it," Mom would say as we dried the last dish and put it in the cupboard. With morning chores complete, out the screen door we ran, eager to enjoy a carefree afternoon while roaming the farm and doing whatever our imaginations conceived. Mom's five directives were: the house is off limits, entertain yourselves, solve your own problems, no tattling, and keep your shoes on. One final directive was that, if we were bored, we could sweep down all the cobwebs in the barn.

Left to our own devices, we were boisterous and inquisitive. Rambling through pastures and woods, we examined wildflowers, observed birds and wild habitat, identified sounds in nature, shouted in the haymow, and skipped rocks in the pond. We were always on the lookout for a four-leaf clover or gold dust. There were unlimited things to explore and interesting stuff to be found. Discarded farm objects and an old junk dump kept us occupied for hours. We could take up one play activity and drop it at any moment for something else that appealed to us more.

We learned many life lessons on those summer afternoons: working out our own problems, negotiating how to get along with each other, and treating each other fairly. Although we bickered, physical violence was not tolerated in our family, and I do not remember any of us engaging in it. We did not tattle on one another because we had learned the futility of being a tattletale; Mom refused to listen anyway.

The Pasture

Mom and Dad warned us repeatedly not to go near the big stock tank of water that the cows drank from. Roving through the pasture, we stuck to the single cow path. Although we collected cockleburs on our socks and pants, we avoided the burning weed and Canadian thistle. Tearing off milkweed leaves, we watched milk ooze onto our hands. Tiny goldfinches perched on purple flower heads of Canadian thistle as we walked along the cattle trail. In August we stopped to admire wild asters and goldenrod. We ambled by lounging cows, some standing, some lying down, flicking their ears and tails to chase away flies as they raised their heads to stare at us and moo before returning to chewing.

The Haymow

To cool off from the blistering afternoon sun, we took cover in the barn, where we could drink the ice-cold water from a hose that ran continually to keep water in the milk cooler cold. The barn, which had a lot of character and was a great place to explore and play, echoed with silence on summer afternoons, except for the buzzing of flies and bees. Filled with hiding places, the barn was a perfect spot for hide-and-seek, especially if we were daring enough to find a hole and cover up with hay.

My siblings and I climbed a ladder of boards nailed to the wall and heaved ourselves through an open hole in the straw loft floor to get to the haymow, one of our favorite places to play. We spent hours upon hours on rainy days and cold winter days playing in the hay and straw mows.

One of the best things about the haymow was a rope that hung from sturdy crossbeams on the ceiling. That simple rope kept us entertained for hours as we jumped from the beams over—or into—the softly mounded hay below.

We climbed to the platform at the east end, our prime launch site, grabbed the rope, took a deep breath, and lunged out across the hay to the wall at the other end of the haymow. After kicking the wall, we flew back across the mountain of hay and lighted on the starting platform. The heavy hay carrier, intended to bring loose hay into the haymow, was anchored on the rail to allow for maximum swinging from one wall to the next. Depending upon your nerve and the amount of hay harvested, this jump could be anywhere from ten to fifteen feet. The trick was to get from the top of the ladder to the center of the narrow beam before jumping.

Over the years, we performed countless flying stunts such as releasing the rope in the middle and falling twenty feet into the hay below. We could have broken an arm or leg—or worse—as we practiced swinging far out into the wide open space of the center barn, but I don't recall any of us ever getting hurt.

The Cupola

On sunny days, we yelled in the empty silo to hear echoes of our voices before going outside to climb the steel tie bars along the silo's wall. Halfway up, we jumped on the slanted barn roof, then we crawled to the peak to perch ourselves next to the cupola where we had a spectacular view of the farm and surrounding fields.

After we tired of the view, we descended and continued wandering. We kicked stones on the gravel driveway, stopped to scratch pigs, and wandered through the empty corncrib. We dared each other to hold a long blade of grass on the electric fence, aware that a jolt would make its way up our arm to our shoulder.

Machine Shed

We entered the machine shed, which smelled of oil and grease, to examine the various items on Dad's workbench: a grease gun, an oil can, pliers, screwdrivers, saws, spades, drills, a hatchet, gopher traps, wrenches, and coffee cans full of nuts, bolts, and nails.

There was a lot to discover in the machinery shed since much had accumulated there over the years. A horse's collar, bridles, a hooded black buggy, a hand-powered fanning mill, and a hand-operated corn sheller were leftovers from the days when horses pulled the machinery. We sat on a metal seat and pedaled a round grindstone mounted on an axle used to sharpen knives. Dad said we were free to play with the "old junk" because it had no value.

The Mysterious Granary

We raced up the five granary steps to check on Warren's ant farm, which was constructed from two old windows. He warned us that a bump might collapse the ant colony's tunnel system.

"Why did you put it in here?" we asked, gathering around to watch the little creatures working in their tunnels and carrying away dead ants.

"It has to be dark so the ants feel like they're underground." Warren said. We concurred because he knew this kind of stuff.

The granary held some mysteries for us kids. Grandma told us that when someone died in winter when the ground was frozen, they would store the body in the bottom of the granary until spring. Dad embellished the truth by telling us that when spring came, the body was gone. It was so easy to believe Dad's stories.

Indian Mounds

Sometimes on a summer afternoon we crossed through the cattle pass, a cement tunnel under a township road that allowed our cattle to walk single file to pastureland on the other side, so we could explore more fields, a haunted island, and a quicksand swamp. Dad warned us that if we ventured too far into the swamp we would disappear into the quicksand. He swore it was true. Believing him, we retrieved cattails and explored around the border, but never risked going too far out.

The island was a place of secrecy, a magic world we entered with trepidation. We speculated that three low rounded hills on the island were Dakota Indian burial mounds, and we marveled that Indians had once pitched tepees and hunted on this land.

Dad said the Indians loved the land and would never damage it. They fished and traded with the settlers. We liked to imagine what it was like for the Indians with no roads, and we discussed what utensils they used for cooking. We even found flint arrowheads on the fields.

"If you dig in burial mounds you will uncover human bones, peace pipes, pottery, and more stuff," Warren told us. "We can't disturb a burial site; it is sacred ground. We better leave these woods alone. Indian spirits live in there. This island is haunted." Many years later, I realized that the stories about the Indian Mounds and quicksand were ideas encouraged by our parents to keep us out of certain places, but at the time we believed what we were told and acted with the proper respect for nature and a culture we didn't fully understand.

The Woods

The woods had many connected trails, which we kids used so often that we wore them into paths. Entering the woods between the house and the pond, we glanced up to see sunlight peek through breaks in the dense ceiling of hardwoods. I savored the solitude of the woods with its cool canopy of interlacing trees. We heard woodland animals before we saw them. A slithering sound alerted us to a garter snake and the rustle of leaves brought our attention to a squirrel or a chipmunk.

Pretending to be Boxcar Children (inspired by the books written by Gertrude Chandler Warner), we cleared brush to transform spaces into houses, outlined rooms with sticks or rocks, constructed furniture of stumps and planks, and searched for treasures to complete our woodland homes. In a dump at the back of the woods, we discovered an old discarded stove, chipped granite pots, utensils, and broken dishes. We cleared pathways from one house to the next and pushed kittens in our doll carriages along these paths.

One day, Warren invited us girls into the heart of the woods to see his "boys'" tree house twenty feet up in a tree. He agreed to build us girls a tree house closer to the ground if we hauled the wood and nails. He showed us how to fasten long string to two tin cans to make a telephone, so we could talk to each other from our respective tree houses.

Mud Pies and the General Store

We made mud pies from sand, clay, seeds, and leaves. Occasionally, we felt compelled to steal a couple of eggs from the brooder house to add to our mud pies, which sat in the sun for several days to bake. We loved to climb trees, but whenever we found a nest with bird's eggs, we heeded Dad's warning not to touch the eggs because our human smell might cause the mother not to return to the nest. Some days we played "general store" on the big porch, using flat green lilac leaves for dollar bills and acorns for quarters, nickels, and dimes. We sold hollyhock petals as doll dresses, Queen Anne's lace as umbrellas, and rhubarb leaves as blankets.

The Pond

We wandered down a well-worn path to the thirty-acre pond to watch turtles basking in the sun on a log. A great blue heron escaped in graceful flight over the pond and, looking up, we marveled at its nest atop a tall tree. We saw muskrat houses, four-foot-high dome-shaped nests of roots, reeds, and mud, partially underwater. A rump sticking up indicated a mallard or a blue-winged teal foraging for food on the bottom of the pond. A streaked brown hen quacked as she encouraged her ducklings to follow her.

Our shoes sank in muck at the edge of the pond while we

searched for flat smooth rocks to skip across the water's surface. I skipped the first one, producing three bounces as it caused the water to ripple. The next toss yielded five bounces. Dad, a gifted stone skipper, told us, "Throw with your wrist, not your arm. It's all in the wrist." Trial and error—and practice—improved our skipping.

A Cattle Dog, Horses, and Tiger-striped Cats

Every farm had a helpful cattle dog. Our lovable long-haired dog was named Jake. He was gentle, and we kids played with him a lot. Animals were not allowed in our house, so Jake spent his life outdoors. We fed him table scraps in the dog dish right outside the backdoor three times a day. Jake went along each summer evening to get the cows for milking time. And he always barked when someone drove into the driveway, which Mom and Dad liked because they were alerted to visitors. If Jake barked at night, Dad went for his gun, assuming some wild animal was after the chickens.

Cats were good pets, too, and good workers as well. Dad said every farm had to have cats to keep the mice population under control. Our tiger-striped cats, all variations of orange, black, gray, and white, always found a good spot in the haymow for having their kittens. We would find them and gently pick them up by the fur on the back of their necks. After we put them back, we knew the mother would move them to a new spot; but we were always able to find them.

Our horses were definitely only for pleasure. Some afternoons we choose to ride Flicka, a high-spirited quarter horse with a white blaze on her forehead. Our other horse was a complacent sandy-colored Shetland pony named Sandy.

Flicka snorted her dissatisfaction when I put a metal bridle bit in her mouth. I saddled her, grabbed the saddle horn, put my foot in the stirrup, and swung myself into the creaking hand-tooled leather saddle. Nearing the end of a ride, Flicka cantered; and soon she galloped, expelling loud heaving noises. Exhilarated and terrified, I could not slow her down as she galloped toward home for food and water.

Occasionally, I was allowed to spend an afternoon with two friends who had horses. We loved to hear the clicking sounds of hooves as we walked our horses on the pavement in Dalton, and we enjoyed racing our horses on the gravel roads outside of town. Flicka loved to race, and she always took the lead.

The little kids rode Sandy, a small brown Shetland pony. He was a babysitter on many washdays when we were too busy working to play with the younger kids. We would plop Daryl on Sandy, and they would circle the house ten or more times. When Sandy got tired of this routine, he trotted down the steep slope of the front yard, stopped abruptly, lowered his head, and Daryl went flying off. Daryl picked himself up without a whimper, and Sandy trotted to the barn for food and water.

Distinguishing Sounds

Stretched out on our backs in the cool green grass, gazing at white fluff drifting across a powder-blue sky, we identified figures in the billowing clouds. Then we closed our eyes to identify sounds.

"I hear a tractor puttering in the field," someone said.

"I hear a cow bellowing and a pig scraping," someone else offered.

"I can hear the telephone wires humming."

"I hear the screen door slamming."

We played this game many days and were adept at identifying poplar leaves fluttering in summer breezes, flies buzzing, a distant woodpecker pecking, and sheets flapping on the clothesline. If the wind blew from the north, we might hear a distant train whistle.

With an innate sense of time, we entered the kitchen at 3:30 to make a pitcher of ice-cold root beer, or orange, cherry, or grape Kool-Aid. We soaked metal trays of ice in hot water and lifted the metal lever, forcing individual dividers to loosen the cubes. Adding one package of powder and one cup of sugar, we filled the pitcher with water and ice cubes. Listening to the whir and creak of the kitchen fan, we sat by the kitchen table and savored our cool drinks and cookies.

"What did you do this afternoon?" Mom asked.

"Nothing," we said contentedly.

Soon lazy summer afternoons gave way to the hustle and bustle of evening chores, bringing cattle home from the pasture and helping Mom prepare supper.

You will go out in joy and be led forth in peace;
the mountains and hills will burst into song before you,
and all the trees of the field will clap their hands.
–Isaiah 55:12 (NIV)

CHAPTER 15

Summer Evenings

Swimming Lessons

There were three things every kid in our community could do: swim, ride a bike, and ice skate. When school let out each spring, we had one week of swimming lessons, which we attended without getting wet. After the ice melted on the lakes, we bused to Pebble Lake outside of Fergus Falls for 9:00 a.m. lessons. We started with fifty jumping jacks, and then we practiced the doggy paddle on shore. We did not get in the water because it was too cold except on the day of the test—even then, the instructors did not get in the water. Anyone in Minnesota knows the first week in June is too cold to swim in lakes, but this was the only week the swim instructors were available.

Once I finally got in the water, I learned to stick my face in and blow bubbles, to not breathe water in, to float on my back, and to make necessary frog-like movements to propel myself along.

With this unconventional way of learning to swim, I became a decent swimmer, never anything fancy, but I figured I could save myself if I fell out of a boat while fishing.

Family Fun

On hot summer evenings, after the barn chores were finished, my entire family piled into our four-door Chevy and headed to the swimming beach on Ten Mile Lake, about five miles from our place. Years later, I realized this was our parents' subtle means of getting us dirty, sweaty kids to bathe.

Our parents positioned themselves under a shady oak tree along the shore, acting as our lifeguards. There was shallow water for the toddlers and an old diving raft further out for us older kids. On the floating platform made of wood and oil barrels we played "king of the platform," or we entertained ourselves with an inner tube from a tractor tire. We never went home without stopping at the small resort store to get ice cream cones.

Returning home, the sound of children's laughter soon filled the yard. While Mom and Dad relaxed under a giant tree in the middle of the front yard, we kids made all kinds of noise as we raced, played games, caught fireflies, or examined the night sky.

Anty Eye Over

Anty Eye Over was a favorite game. We divided into two teams, one on either side of the house, over which we tossed a ball and shouted, "Anty eye over." If an attempt to throw the ball over the house was unsuccessful, we yelled "Pig's tail!" and tried again. If the team on the other side caught the ball, they split up so that the opposing team did not know who had the ball. They then ran around the house in both directions, attempting to tag opponents by throwing the ball at them. Wild screams ensued whenever a surprise runner jumped out from behind a tree to tag a thrower.

Kick the Can

Next we might place a coffee can in the front yard to play Kick the Can. The person picked to guard the can counted to one hundred while the rest of us scattered and found places to hide. When done counting, the guard tried to find and tag us before we got to the can and kicked it. Captured players sat on the grass by Mom and Dad, but they were set free when someone else kicked the can.

Star Light, Star Bright

When it got dark, we often played "Star Light, Star Bright, I Hope to See a Ghost Tonight." The "ghost" hid while the rest of us stood on the front step and counted to fifty. When we reached fifty, we ran around the house hollering "Star Light, Star Bright, I hope to see a ghost tonight." The ghost tried to tag us before we made it around the house and to the front step. We let out a bloodcurdling scream whenever the ghost closed in on us.

Fireflies and Constellations

By the east yard tree line, we saw fireflies blinking their lights as they flew. We caught them in canning jars and set them free before plopping on the grass by Mom and Dad. Laughter gave way to quiet discussions and challenges to find the Little Dipper, Big Dipper, and other constellations. If we were really lucky, we would see a falling star and make a wish.

Time to Hit the Hay

Dad yawned and stood up. "As much as I enjoy your laughter, I think it is time to hit the hay."

After we were in bed and the lights were turned off, we girls conversed across the hall to the boys in their room. Soon roars of laughter filled the air; and, as anticipated, Dad yelled up the stairs, "That's enough yakking up there. There's work to be done tomorrow." We knew then it was time to be quiet.

On summer nights we kept our windows open to allow the breezes to waft through. We heard crickets and frogs, along with the occasional bawl of a cow or squeal of a pig. If the moon shone bright in our windows, we quietly constructed shadow shapes on the wall. The whispering soon ceased, and we fell asleep listening to the night crickets and frogs.

He makes me lie down in green pastures,
he leads me beside quiet waters,
–Psalm 23:2 (NIV)

Kids with Grandma and Grandpa Nagle

CHAPTER 16

Fishing, Hunting, and Trapping

Although Dad did not believe in abusing or mistreating animals, he felt it was okay to hunt if we used what we caught for meat or clothing. His exceptions were the animals that were destroying his crops, such as blackbirds and gophers. He told the story that his father had told him about how David in the Old Testament had to kill a lion and a bear to protect his sheep as part of his shepherd's duty.

We lived in an environment conducive to hunting and fishing. Dad insisted that even his daughters learn to shoot and carry a rifle. We cared little for hunting or guns, but we enrolled in the Youth Firearm Safety Class and received our patches. The only things I ever shot were old soup cans.

Since it was inappropriate for a girl to own a gun, we started with Warren's BB gun. Dad purchased pellets, and we poured them into a special opening in the gun. I learned to cup my fingers around the hole to make a funnel for the tiny BBs. The barrel reservoir held many BBs, which rolled around when we raised or lowered the gun. Holding the barrel upright for a BB to enter the firing chamber, we gave a single hard pull on the cocking lever to set the trigger. Bringing the gun up to eye level, I heard Dad say, "You're shutting the wrong eye."

Pheasant Hunting

We girls went pheasant hunting, but we never carried a gun. For whatever reason, we agreed to flush pheasants for Dad and Warren to shoot. We drudged through rows of corn, and walked fence lines and field edges in hopes of rousing birds. The thrill was in hearing the whir of a ring-necked pheasant's wings beating and to watch it flush straight in front of us.

"Look for three-toed tracks," Dad told us as we prepared for the hunt. "Pheasants will freeze when they first see and hear you. They will try to escape by running, and finally they will take flight. That's when we fire."

Trapping Gophers

"Do you kids want to earn a little extra cash this week?" Dad asked.

"Yes!" we all shouted.

"Well, I noticed several low dirt mounds in the east field—signs of the gophers that are eating our plant roots. If you want to dig out the gopher traps, you could make yourselves a little extra cash. The township board pays a twenty-five cent bounty for a pocket gopher tail and a ten-cent bounty for a striped gopher tail."

Armed with metal traps and chains, stakes to hold the chains in place, and a shovel, we commenced on our mission. Listening for the gophers' high-pitched whistle and looking for the flick of their tails, we focused our energy on checking the mounds of fresh dirt.

"Here's a fresh mound," I hollered, burrowing to find a tunnel.

"Set the trap at the entrance of the tunnel," Warren instructed. "And don't forget to hook the chain to the metal stake so he won't be able to drag the trap into his home."

After covering the entrance to block out light, we placed the rest of our traps.

"I am going to put gopher tails in my church envelope," Warren said a few days later.
"They're worth tens cents apiece."

"Oh no, you're not," Mom said. "Where do you come up with these ideas?"

"That's what they did in *Gopher Tales for Papa*," Warren said. "Dad thinks it's a sensible idea."

"Over my dead body," Mom told him. "Next thing I know, you'll be throwing pop bottles in the collection plate."

"You should read the book, Mom. It's a wonderful way to collect money."

"Absolutely not," Mom said. "And that's final."

Scaring Away Blackbirds

On fall evenings, thousands of red-winged blackbirds blackened the sky when returning to roost in the cattail stands in our low wetland marsh.

"I'll buy as many shells as you want to shoot, if you try to frighten them from our cornfields," Dad said. "But it needs to be in early morning or late afternoon when they're feeding on corn."

"Doesn't do any good," said Warren.

"I think you're right about that," Dad replied. "I read in *Successful Farmer* about propane exploders. Maybe we should give them a try."

"Maybe we shouldn't plant corn next to the slough," Warren suggested.

"Well, they don't only eat corn from that field. They fly to fields within five miles of the slough roosts."

"I think we have to figure out how to get rid of the slough."

"It's not as easy to tile and drain as you think. You have to get the cooperation of neighbors."

Muskrat Fur

Muskrats built homes on our pond, and the boys earned extra cash trapping them in winter. Before and after school, they walked on ice to the muskrats' four-foot-high, dome-shaped nest of roots, reeds, and mud on the slough. Using the gopher traps, they trapped the muskrats for their soft, thick fur, which they sold for $3.50 a pelt.

Rods and Reels

On a windy, overcast spring or summer evening, Dad would announce, "This is a perfect evening to fish for walleyes. Who wants to catch a whopper?" Dad permitted two or three of us to tag along, under the condition we scavenge a coffee can full of angleworms.

Carting rods and reels, a stringer for our catch, and worms, we piled in a wooden boat with four wooden slats to sit on, powered by a five-horsepower outboard motor rented at Ten Mile

Lake resort. Launching off, Dad navigated to his special walleye location. He cut the engine and baited hooks for us girls. "Drop your line in the water and set your bobber," Dad told us. "I think we're going to get big ones tonight."

As the boat swayed in choppy waters, not many words passed between us because we didn't want to scare the fish. "I've got a big one," Dad teased as he stood and pretended to tug on his line. "Get the big net!"

We glanced at his empty line.

"Too late," Dad said as he sat down. "It got away. It was a ten pounder, for sure!"

Suddenly, my red-and-white bobber went under. Something was on my line. I waited until the bobber went all the way underwater, jerked the line, and reeled in an olive-and gold-colored fish with large staring eyes. I realized I caught a walleye when I saw the white belly flap around in the boat. Dad detached the hook from its mouth with his pliers.

The thrill of a bobber going under, and the gentle sound of waves hitting our boat, made fishing a wonderful experience. Dad pulled up the anchor and moved to a new spot, until finally he said, "That's enough action for today. Reel in your lines."

Ice Fishing

Dark-house spear fishing scared me, but I tagged along when it was my turn. Looking apprehensive, Dad guided his pickup truck across a frozen lake to his dark house while my gut wrenched, scared the ice would break. Dad steered the truck with the doors partway open, in case we needed to jump.

"A polar bear can crawl out of an ice hole, and you're smarter than a bear," Dad said, trying to calm me.

A terrifying conviction in my stomach worsened as I crossed the threshold of Dad's windowless ten-foot-square dark house. A mammoth four-foot square hole encompassed the floor. The first thing we had to do was remove the ice chunks and chips from the hole. Dad parked himself on a stool. When a northern pike darted by, Dad slowly lifted the heavy spear, took aim, and dropped the spear onto the fish. A rope tied to the spear let him retrieve the fish.

As I moved to my stool, I clutched a wall, lest I lose my footing and plunge into the hole. A lake cavity provided our light. As Dad braced to spear another Northern, I considered what to do if I toppled through the opening. Warren said to edge your way along the air between the ice and water until you came to an opening. Wiggling my frozen toes in my four-buckle boots, I thought about how long I could stay alive breathing those pockets of air.

Although none of us girls became hunters or fishers, we relish our memories of time with Dad spent fishing on a quiet lake, reminiscing about big ones that got away, and feeling special.

Now then, get your equipment—your quiver and bow—and go out to the open country to hunt some wild game for me.
–Genesis 27:3 (NIV)

CHAPTER 17

High Card Deals

When we were old enough to sit on a chair and see over the top of the table, Mom and Dad taught us the rudiments of card games, beginning with games of chance and progressing to games of skill. Before we knew how to count, we recognized spades, hearts, clubs, and diamonds; and our first counting memories emerged as "ace, king, queen, jack, ten, nine, eight, seven, six, five, and four." War, Concentration, Slap Jack, Solitaire, and Old Maid were predictable; while Crazy Eights, Rummy, Canasta, and Rook required keen watchfulness and memory. Cribbage demanded excellent pegging skills.

Since we did not own a television, winter evenings were often devoted to playing cards. Most of us developed a passion for whist equal to our parents. Before settling into our places at the kitchen table, we drew cards to determine partners, with Mom and Dad on opposing teams. We followed simple whist rules: shuffle, cut, deal thirteen cards to each person, bid a black card for high, a red one for low, grand with thirteen points, and count the cards played in each suit. We learned to finesse, bluff, count points, mislead, dupe our opponents, and read our partner's face.

Ribbing and good-natured bantering ensued between Mom and Dad. Mom's extrajudicial nature and Dad's teasing became a constant element of the game.

"Man, am I loaded with big fellows," Dad grinned as he sorted his suits.

"Milton, that's talking in the cards," Mom said.

"If you have the cards, don't be scared to bid high," Dad informed his partner. "You only have to take seven tricks, and you have a partner."

"Milton, that's unwarranted."

"Just lead out with an ace."

"Milton, that's uncalled for."

"Remember to play your partner's hand."

"Milton, that's inexcusable."

"Don't forget who has played what now."

"Milton, quit talking in the cards."

"You're not playing this alone—remember, you have a partner."

"Oh, for crying out loud! That's cheating," Mom said.

"It's a game. Why get so upset?" Dad asked innocently.

"Thank God I don't have a drop of Norwegian blood in me," Mom mumbled.

"What's that awful smell in here?" Dad teased if his team skunked the other team.

Cribbage

Then there was *cribbage,* a card game where the score is kept with little pegs on a cribbage board. Most of our pegs were lost, so we used matches as pegs.

"Fifteen-two, fifteen-four, fifteen-six, and a pair make eight."

The cribbage board sat out all winter and was ready for Dad whenever he came in for a break.

Board Games

Board games were popular in our family because we did not have a television and everyone could play. Our supply of games included Monopoly, Sorry, Parcheesi, Cootie, Go to the Head of the Class, Tiddlywinks, Yahtzee, Checkers, and Clue. We older children spent hours playing Candy Land and Chutes and Ladders with the little ones.

Gathering around the kitchen table for a game of Monopoly, we divided play money into piles and arranged the properties and the Chance and Community Chest cards. As the game progressed, we kids bantered boisterously.

When Mom got tired of the noise and bickering, she opened the dining room door and said, "Everyone outside NOW."

"Why?" we said.

"Because I said so, that's why."

"We weren't fighting. We were discussing the rules."

"If I've told you once, I've told you a hundred times. The babies are sleeping. Now get outside. And shut the door behind you."

Carrom and Other Games

We played Carrom on a large square board of lacquered plywood with a checkers pattern, wooden bumpers, and net pockets in the corners. Snapping a shooter with our finger, we attempted to flick an opponent's wooden ring into one of four corners. To this day, I am amazed at how hard Dad could snap the shooter with his fingernail.

We also played several games that children still play today, such as hide-and-seek, baseball, jump rope, tag, and hopscotch. In addition, we made up our own games, too.

Word Games

We became adept at mixing play with work. While digging silage or throwing hay down from the loft, we made up word games and mind challenges.

"Let's play the alphabet plant game," someone shouted. "It has to be a plant on our farm."

Someone yelled, "A is for alfalfa, asters, and astilbe."

Someone followed with "B is for balloon flower, bleeding hearts, black-eyed Susan, and baby's breath."

Sometimes the challenge was to name a bird for every letter of the alphabet. To make the challenge harder we decided it had to be a bird on our farm: blackbird, bluebird, cardinal, chickadee, crow, coot, dove, duck, eagle, egret, finch, goldfinch, goose, gull, hawk, hen, hummingbird, heron, jay, killdeer, lark, mallard, meadowlark, nuthatch, oriole, owl, pelican, pheasant, robin, sparrow, swallow, woodpecker, or wren.

Some days it was naming trees on the farm: apple, ash, box elder, elm, maple, oak, pine, plum, or spruce. It might be listing boys' or girls' names with each letter of the alphabet. Another challenge was naming farm equipment: auger, baler, combine, corn picker, cultivator, drill, elevator, harrow, hay cutter, hayrack, manure spreader, planter, plow, rake, stone boat, swatter, tractor, and wagon.

If we had been studying homonyms in school, we challenged each other to name as many as we could. Sometimes we named all the states and capitals or continents and countries.

Gender-specific Toys

We got store-bought toys and games once a year, on Christmas. Gender identification was a natural component of our childhood. At school, girls played with girls and boys with boys. Even at home, gender stereotyping was evident: boys were encouraged to play with toy tractors and such; while girls had dolls, tea sets, and dollhouses. Ant farms and chemistry sets were marketed to boys, since girls were not going to grow up to be scientists (or so it seemed).

Our dolls were very special to us girls. We each had one, and Grandma often sewed a dress for our doll with leftover scraps of material from the dresses she made for us.

However, there were some toys that all of us kids played with: Tonka trucks, Lincoln Logs, and Tinkertoys lasted through all eight children. Likewise, an Etch-a-Sketch and a View-Master were bought once and shared by all.

Always try to be kind to each other and to everyone else.
–1 Thessalonians 5:15 (NIV)

CHAPTER 18

Winter Fun

While summer provided ample opportunity for us to explore and have adventures, the cold and snow of winter allowed for plenty of entertaining activities, too. Whether playing games, using our imaginations, or being athletic, we had no shortage of ways to stay busy, even in the coldest months.

Snow Forts, Tunnels, and King of the Hill

When winter's first significant snowfall arrived, Dad cleared our front yard with a tractor and bucket, piling snow into ten-foot mounds. We bundled up in layers of clothing, donned our long johns, snow pants, boots with thick felt liners, hats, mittens, and scarves, and ventured outside for fun in the snow.

Using a shovel and our hands, we dug tunnels in the huge snow piles and built protective snow forts for anticipated snowball altercations. The first surprise snowball usually came from Dad, while he was hiding behind a tree. I do not recall anyone ever getting hurt in a snowball fight, but I do remember that it was always Warren and Daryl against us three girls.

Warren stood on top of the highest snow pile, taunting, "I'm king of the hill!" Audrey, Jo, and I rushed up the hill, struggling to toss him from the top position onto the mound of snow below. He pushed us, kicked us, and tossed us off the hill. Screaming and laughing, we tumbled down the slopes. Next, we girls scrambled up on three sides in a valiant attempt to take control of the highest snow hill in our land.

Radio Flyer Sleds

Spirits soared as we hurled down our favorite hill on our Radio Flyer sleds. The front of the sled moved back and forth to make steering easy as we raced, icy air filling our lungs and a spray of snow hitting our faces. We competed until we spilled, and then, clutching the sled rope, we climbed the hill, leaving a trail from the red metal runners. On our second run, we coasted facing backwards, bailed out before hitting a ditch; and once again we clambered up the hill to repeat the sport.

Fox and Geese

"Let's play Fox and Geese," someone hollered as they tramped down the snow to make a large circle with eight spokes and a small circle in the middle. One person was the fox and the rest of us kids were geese. The fox tried to tag the geese "out" by chasing us up and down the spokes and around the rim. If we were tagged, we became the fox and the game started over.

Snow Angels and Snowmen

Lying on our backs in the snow, we moved our arms and legs in a jumping jack motion to make snow angels. The secret was to carefully stand up without ruining the design.

Next, we rolled wet and heavy snow to build a snowman. Stacking heavy snowballs atop one another, we wedged them together with snow. After placing the last snowball for a snowman's head, we carved out arms and attached big ears made of snow to turn our three-circle snowman into a cartoon character or a person. Two pieces of coal were added for eyes and a stick for the nose.

Ice Skating

Much of our winter play involved ice skating. We used two skating rinks—the one at school and the pond behind the barn. The swish of my sharpened blades cutting clean edges in the ice was an exhilarating sound to me.

Sometime in December, after a spell of cold weather, Dad established that the ice on the slough was thick enough for us to safely skate on it. We trekked through the knee-high snow in the woods to the pond with our sharpened skates slung over our shoulders, perched ourselves on a log, removed our mittens, pulled our skates over two pair of wool socks, and tightened the laces.

"Are you sure it's safe?" I asked as I teetered out onto the ice, the sky clear and the weather cold.

"Of course—Dad said so," Warren said as he glided past me.

Although I trusted Dad, I had reservations about the ice. A groaning sound alerted me to danger, but Dad said the ice makes that sound as it hardens.

I skated forward, my skates crossing one in front of the other, made a precise turn, and created a crisp sound as my metal blades came to a stop. Skating backward, I carved figure eights into the fresh ice.

"Let's play tag," Jo said, skating by as she tagged me. "You're it."

I circled, weaved, and tagged Audrey, "You're it."

We all linked hands for Crack the Whip, pulled by Warren at the lead, and picked up speed. Experience taught us he would let go and we would all land on our butts.

The other ice-skating rink we used was the one on the school grounds. Every winter the northeast end of the playground was edged with banks of snow and flooded to make a skating rink. A warming house was available, where we put on and took off our skates. Sometimes when I stayed with Grandma, I would call a couple friends who lived in town, and we would skate at night. The rink was softly lit; and if it wasn't too cold, it was truly beautiful to skate under the stars.

Were You Born in a Barn?

When we could barely feel our fingertips and toes after an afternoon or evening of sledding or ice skating, with our mittens soaked, frost on the scarves tied around our face, and our pants legs frozen stiff to our knees, we headed for the house to warm up. The sound of boots stomping on the front porch alerted Mom to begin making hot cocoa.

"Shut the door," Mom scolded. "Were you born in a barn?"

An array of soggy mittens drying on the woodstove and the warmth of a steamy kitchen is a cherished memory.

Rejoice always,
–1 Thessalonians 5:16 (NIV)

Treasured Encyclopedias

CHAPTER 19

Hardcover Friends

Reading was a big part of our childhoods. Learning to read, like learning to talk, evolved naturally. Dad and Mom, being prolific readers, ingrained the love of reading and learning in us early. Although we did not have an ample supply of children's literature in our home, we made do with farm journals, the daily newspaper, our parents' Reader's Digest Condensed Books, our *World Book Encyclopedia*, and the school library.

Little Golden Books

Our relationship with reading started with the Little Golden Books. Mom purchased the gold-foil-bound paperboard books for twenty-five cents apiece. I read and reread *The Three Bears, Tootle, The Happy Family*, and *Santa's Toy Shop*. To the little kids, I read *The Poky Little Puppy, Three Little Kittens, Mother Goose, The Little*

Red Hen, The Animals of Farmer Jones, and *This Little Piggy.*

Perhaps our favorite Little Golden Book was *Little Black Sambo.* Sambo is a black boy who encounters four hungry tigers. One by one, Sambo sheds his shoes, jacket, pants, and umbrella so the tigers won't eat him. The vain tigers then chase each other around a tree until they are reduced to melted butter. Sambo gets his clothes back and takes the butter home to his mother to make pancakes. Eventually, use of the word "Sambo" was considered a racial slur to black children, and the original *Little Black Sambo* book was no longer published.

World Book Encyclopedias

A 1947 set of the *World Book Encyclopedia* reigned as the focal point in our living room. A few years after those reference books were purchased, a traveling salesman convinced Mom and Dad that our school reports would be inaccurate if we used such obsolete material, so Dad sold a load of wheat to purchase the new 1960 set of the *World Book Encyclopedia* and a fourteen-volume set of Childcraft books. This was by far the most expensive gift we ever received, and the most cherished.

Being inquisitive, we searched the encyclopedias for answers to Dad's probing questions and for responses to queries we formulated while spending afternoons doing chores or playing in nature. Warren used the encyclopedias as he challenged and debated issues and questioned our parents and teachers. We girls used the encyclopedias to prove Warren wrong.

Dad cautioned us that encyclopedias contain facts rather than wisdom. Wisdom, he said, is more than knowledge or intelligence; it is being able to apply knowledge. He often teased, "If there is a tractor fire, Warren will run to an encyclopedia to determine how to put it out, while Daryl will run for a bucket of water."

The Daily Newspaper

On weekdays the entire family perused the *Fergus Falls Daily Journal.* We kids jostled to be first to rifle through the funnies and see what advice Ann Landers had to offer. Dad examined the world news, and Mom glanced at the local news and wedding announcements. On Sundays we skimmed the *Minneapolis Star and Tribune* and passed around the "funny papers."

The Farm Journal

Magazines were another favorite reading material. Mom and Dad subscribed to *Reader's Digest, Farm Journal, The Farmer,* and *Successful Farmer.* Dad scrutinized the farm magazines to learn the latest techniques in farming, while we girls and Mom examined the recipe sections. I read *Reader's Digest* from cover to cover.

I learned a valuable lesson from Dad as he read his farm journals to discover the latest and best methods of farming. His philosophy was that you can't believe everything you read and that it is good to challenge ideas, but not people. He always looked to see if the author was an authentic farmer writing about his actual experience and judgment honed in the field. Even then, he always applied his critical mind to the new information to see if it fit with what he already knew about raising livestock and crops.

Reader's Digest Condensed Books

During the summer months we had little access to books, as Dalton did not have a public library. I picked any book in the house just to have something to read. I reread *The Bobbsey Twins*, Nancy Drew mystery stories, *Heidi*, *The Black Stallion*, Trixie Belden mysteries, and other books we had received as presents. We ransacked our parents' bookshelves. They belonged to the Reader's Digest Condensed Book Club, and four times a year received a volume in the mail containing four or five condensed books. Having no choice but to read indiscriminately, these became our summer reading. I discovered William Faulkner, John Steinbeck, Pearl S. Buck, and Winston Churchill. I read *The Caine Mutiny* by Herman Wouk, *Gone with the Wind* by Margaret Mitchell, *East of Eden* by John Steinbeck, and *Onions in the Stew* by Betty MacDonald.

The School Library

For the nine months we were in school each year, we had unlimited access to books from the school library. Because we did not have a television and did not take trips, books were the primary source of broadening my perception of the world.

I first became aware that friends lived in books when my first-grade teacher, Mrs. Halvorson, read *Blueberries for Sal*, *Millions of Cats*, *Make Way for Ducklings*, and *The Five Chinese Brothers*. I remember with delight reading *The Story About Ping* by Marjorie Flack and Kurt Wiese. I recall Ping not wanting to be the last duck on the boat, because he would get a smack on the back from the master of the boat. Two other sets of books that I adored were by a Swedish author, Maj Lindman. One series was about Swedish triplet boys named Snipp, Snapp, and Snurr, and the other was about triplet girls named Flicka, Ricka, and Dicka.

Mrs. Halvorson also read us *The Boxcar Children*, a story about four orphan siblings trying to survive on their own. Many afternoons in the playhouse in our woods at home, my siblings and

I role-played this story. Warren was Henry, I was Jessie, Audrey was Violet, Jo was Benny, and our dog Jake was Watch.

Newberry Medal and Honor Books

One of my goals in grade school was to read all of the Newberry Medal and Honor books. Because of our limited cultural experiences, reading helped us understand other people. I felt loneliness, injustice, discrimination, love, and courage as I read books. These stories and the characters in them offered me love, friendship, and humor. They allowed me to escape to new and imaginary places. The themes and subjects that mattered to me most were family, survival, independence, and human kindness.

I remember reading the historical fiction book *The Witch of Blackbird Pond* by Elizabeth George Speare for the first time when I was in the sixth grade. It was haunting. The story dealt with charges of witchcraft in a Puritan community. I cried for the beautiful Kit because no one loved her except the elderly Hannah Tupper, who people considered a witch.

In *Caddie Woodlawn* by Carol Ryrie Brink, I admired the title character's penchant for expressing herself, doing what she felt was right, and her love of nature. I rejoiced when she got revenge on a snobbish, visiting cousin. And in *The Hundred Dresses* by Eleanor Estes, I felt Wanda's pain when the kids bullied her.

I read and reread the *Little House on the Prairie* series by Laura Ingalls Wilder because they were about human kindness and family. I felt a rousing sense of independence while reading *The Courage of Sarah Nobel,* and I roared with laughter while reading *Pippi Longstocking.* I wanted to be as independent as Pippi.

But no book left as powerful and lasting an impression on me as Scott O'Dell's *Island of the Blue Dolphins.* The story, about

survival and independence, is about what happens to a young girl
and her brother who are left to live alone on an island.

To these four young men God gave knowledge and understanding
of all kinds of literature and learning.
And Daniel could understand visions and dreams of all kinds.
–Daniel 1:17 (NIV)

PART FIVE

Family Folkways

Maxine's Sixth Birthday

CHAPTER 20

Irish Relatives

They drank tea instead of coffee. They ate dandelion greens and not lefse. They hired seasonal migratory workers from Mexico to plant and harvest their sugar beet crops. For a non-worldly Norwegian girl from Minnesota, visiting my Irish grandparents in North Dakota provided my first exposure to a different culture.

My mother's parents, Rose and Walter Nagle, were Irish Catholic immigrants whose ancestors settled in Ontario before moving to rural Manvel, North Dakota, in 1878. Every summer my grandparents drove from North Dakota in a black Model T Ford to visit us. Grandpa brought us a sack of bran, advising us to put it in our morning oatmeal to keep us "regular," and Grandma delivered a homemade goose-down pillow.

A pillar of strength and a tenacious Catholic, Grandma Rose was austere and determined. She sat in a chair while patching jeans and darning socks, conversing all the while with Mom about events back home. Grandpa solemnly walked the farmstead and often wandered into Mom's garden to pull weeds.

The Summer Railroad Trip

Ten years old, I stood alone at the Great Northern Railway station in Fergus Falls and waited to board a train traveling westward. I fought back tears as I boarded for my one-week summer visit to Manvel, North Dakota. Although Grandma and Grandpa Nagle were congenial people, visiting them was like stepping into a different culture. I dreaded this visit to grandparents who were essentially strangers, knowing I would experience a gut-wrenching feeling of loneliness.

For three hours I stared out the train window, fearful I would miss the Grand Forks stop; the train also stopped at Barnesville, Fargo, and Hillsboro. I heard the porter announce, "Grand Forks, next exit." Grandma and Grandpa met me in their two-door Model T Ford pickup, and we made our way down gravel roads to their Red River Valley farm where they raised sugar beets.

They had no electricity, running water, or telephone. Kerosene lamps mandated we go to bed when the sun went down. A pail of water stood on the cupboard with a dipper in it for drinking. Grandma toasted a slice of bread by putting it on a fork and holding it over the fire.

Every night after supper, we knelt to say the rosary. A long narrow porch with walls of windows ran across the front of the house, where we sat in the evening.

Being intrusive, I asked Grandma as many questions as she would permit. "Grandma, tell me about Mom when she was little."

"Your mom, sixth of our eight children, was delivered by a midwife right in this house."

"Where did she go to school?"

"She started first grade at age five, walking two miles to school with her brothers and sisters. In cold North Dakota winters, Walter occasionally drove them to the one-room schoolhouse in a buggy or sleigh pulled by horses. I heated bricks and wrapped them in blankets to keep their feet warm. Your mom carried an empty syrup pail with a sandwich, cookies, and fruit for lunch. After school, she would help with various chores such as husking corn for pigs or doing dishes.

"She wore a dress to school, and I sewed each of my girls a new dress twice a year: one for the first day of school and one for Christmas. We purchased underwear through the Sears or Montgomery Ward mail-order catalogs, same as you do.

"They rode in our horse-drawn buggy or sleigh to St. Timothy's Catholic Church every Sunday, and after church nuns instructed them on the Baltimore Catechism."

Grandma sighed as she reached for her prayer book. "I think that is enough questions for one day."

Upstairs were two bedrooms. I slept in one, and Grandma and Grandpa slept in the other one. I remember crying myself to sleep because I was so lonesome.

Love never fails.
–1 Corinthians 13:8 (NIV)

CHAPTER 21

Feed Sack Dresses

With eight kids to clothe, Mom embraced the motto "repair, reuse, make do, and don't throw anything away." Grandma and Mom knew how to use everything and not be wasteful. Mom sewed patches over holes in clothes. Grandma lengthened hems. Younger siblings "made do" with hand-me-downs. My older brother remembers most of his clothes coming from an older cousin in Grand Forks. When clothes could no longer be mended, the buttons were cut off to be reused and the fabrics were saved for making rugs or used as rags for cleaning.

When Dad brought home big sacks of flour, livestock feed, or chicken feed, Grandma used the printed cotton muslin sacks as material to sew dresses and shirts for Mom and us kids, as well as blouses, pillowcases, aprons, and kitchen towels. The sacks came in floral, checked, or plaid prints.

We had three categories of clothes: farm clothes, school

clothes, and dress clothes. Our clothes came from one of three places: Grandma sewed them, we ordered them from a mail order catalogue, or we wore hand-me-downs.

While working and playing on the farm, we dressed like ragamuffins in farm clothes. We were not concerned about wearing a striped top with plaid bottoms. For hauling hay, we wore long sleeves and long pants because the stubble was itchy. For winter barn chores, we donned long underwear, wool socks, scarves, a barn coat, and four-buckle black boots over our shoes. In the heat of summer, we wore pedal pushers or shorts and sleeveless blouses.

Changing into farm clothes was the first thing we did when we got home from school. The second thing we did was make jelly sandwiches for our afternoon snack. Then we began our chores. For morning barn chores, not wanting our hair to smell like the barn, we wore dishtowels tied turban-style at the forehead.

For school, we dressed the same as the other kids in our community. Our fashion guidelines came from the models in the Sears Roebuck catalogue. We girls wore cotton slacks to school. If we wore a dress we had to wear slacks under the dress when we went outside. I do not remember why, but we always wore undershirts.

We never needed more than one dressy outfit at a time. We received a new outfit for Easter and one for Christmas, and we wore those for church and social events for the remainder of the year. Black patent leather Mary Jane shoes with a strap, along with a hat and gloves, completed our outfits for church. We wore circle skirts with stiff petticoats called can-cans, which we stiffened with sugar and water.

Grandma's Dressmaking

Grandma delighted in sewing dresses, jumpers, and blouses for her granddaughters. She started with the floral or checked feed sack material and then added ruffles, lace, and rickrack. As her assistant, I straightened out the small drawers of bobbins, thread, thimbles, basting tape, pins, and fabric to help keep everything organized.

With her mouth full of straight pins, Grandma measured patterns against my torso. Spreading the fabric on the kitchen table, she pinned a McCall's, Butterick, or Simplicity pattern to the fabric before cutting it with her pinking shears. Her Singer sewing machine was powered by a large foot pedal—the faster she pumped, the faster she sewed. Soon she requested that I stand on a chair while she checked for straight seams, even darts, and proper hem length. Grandma made our dresses with a good-size hem on them so they could be lengthened as we grew taller. I cherished the dresses Grandma made more than any catalogue-ordered dress. With extra material, she made a dress for a younger sister or a doll.

Mail Order Catalogs

Each fall before school, we selected underpants, undershirts, knee-highs, anklets, and black-and-white saddle shoes from the Sears Roebuck, JC Penney, or Montgomery Ward mail order catalogues. In the catalogue, there was even a page where we could measure our feet to determine what size to order.

Gingham Aprons and Housedresses

Grandma and Mom wore cotton housedresses with gingham aprons over them to keep the dresses clean. Grandma made beautiful aprons with chicken scratch embroidery. After the 1960s, my mother started to wear pantsuits, but Grandma never donned a pair of slacks during her life.

Women wore dress gloves and hats for church and carried a purse with a hanky in it. Mom and Grandma finished off their outfits with clip-on earrings and Evening in Paris cologne.

Toni Home Perm

Most of the time we girls wore a bob, but occasionally Mom would give us a Toni home permanent. She was able to stretch the waving lotion and reuse the tissue squares so all three of us girls could get a perm from one kit. Enduring the smell of the milky solution was a whole lot easier than enduring the pain of Mom wrapping each strand of hair around a pink plastic curler. Truth be told, we never got curls—we got frizz. We set our hair with wave set and bobby pins.

Therefore I tell you, do not worry about your life,
what you will eat or drink; or about your body, what you will wear.
Is not life more than food, and the body more than clothes?
Look at the birds of the air; they do not sow or reap or store away
in barns, and yet your heavenly Father feeds them.
Are you not much more valuable than they?
Can any one of you by worrying add a single hour to your life?
–Matthew 6:25–27 (NIV)

CHAPTER 22

Cod Liver Oil

Mom said she always wanted to be a nurse, and taking care of our health was something she took seriously. Her first and foremost health rule was that we always have shoes on our feet. She was constantly worried that we would step on a rusty nail or a piece of glass as we roamed the farm. I never remember going without shoes.

The second thing Mom worried about was that one of the little ones would drown in the big watering tank for livestock. If ever a child went missing, Mom immediately ran for the stock tank. Because of this fear, she made everyone take swimming lessons.

My mother kept current on health matters. The door-to-door Watkins salesman, rather than a doctor, convinced Mom that cod liver oil provided an excellent nutritional supplement and prevented illness. Therefore, each winter evening before bed we lined up (oldest to youngest) and gulped one teaspoon of the detestable, sardine-smelling tonic, followed by a saltine cracker to get rid of the taste.

Home remedies were employed when we contracted standard illnesses such as a sore throat, the chicken pox, measles, and the flu. If we were congested or had a sore throat, the remedy was to rub a liberal amount of Mentholatum ointment on your neck and then wrap a wool sock around your throat. If babies were cranky when getting new teeth, we rubbed whiskey on their gums. Butter soothed burns, alum and saltwater cured canker sores, an orange rubber hot water bottle alleviated cramps, calamine lotion relieved itching, and Alka Seltzer cured upset stomachs. A cold washcloth placed on the forehead brought down fever, though we usually just crawled under blankets to sweat it out. To disinfect cuts and scratches, **Mom used** Mercurochrome, which came in a tiny brown bottle with a glass dropper to apply the medicine. As I recall, it had a terrible sting to it.

Polio

The early '50s was a time of fear because polio stalked the country, crippling and killing children, and everyone knew someone who got it. Polio was a frightening viral disease that afflicted tens of thousands of people. In 1955 Dr. Jonas Salk developed a vaccine for polio. I was in first grade. The county nurses came to our school and gave us the vaccination.

Dentist

We brushed our teeth daily at home; but of course, we did not have fluoride in the well water. Once a year, we each had a dentist appointment, with a dentist in Elbow Lake. The only time we went to the dentist in an emergency was when applications of iodine and peroxide did not remedy tooth pain. Pulling the back molars was as likely to take place as filling them. I hated going to the dentist with a passion, a fear I am sure was overly exaggerated.

Daryl and the Sow

One summer, Dad assigned five-year-old Daryl to haul corncobs in his Red Flyer wagon from the corncrib to the pen, with strict orders to throw the cobs over the fence and stay out of the pen. One morning, Daryl noticed that a sow had delivered a litter, and he crawled over the fence to hold a piglet. The protective sow attacked Daryl. Warren and Dad heard screaming from the barn and ran there immediately. They pulled Daryl from the pen—he was covered in blood. Wrapping his bleeding head, Mom hollered at me to finish the laundry as she and Dad drove to the Fergus Falls hospital, with Daryl screaming and crying. A couple hours later, Mom and Dad returned with Daryl. He boasted about the thirteen stitches he'd received on top of his head. This incident did not make us scared of the pigs on the farm; rather, we learned about the natural protective instinct of a new mother sow.

A joyful heart is good medicine,
But a broken spirit dries up the bones.
–Proverbs 17:22 (NIV)

PART SIX

Holidays

Fourth of July Picnic

CHAPTER 23

Fourth of July Picnic

When I was a youngster, we went on a picnic every July 4, regardless of anything short of a cloudburst. While Mom fried three large chickens in two black skillets and put them in the oven to bake, I peeled and sliced potatoes to fill a large casserole for scalloped potatoes made with our heavy cream and butter.

We packed three rhubarb pies, scalloped corn, homemade buns, lemonade, plates, glasses, and silverware. We also brought along old blankets to sit on, towels for swimming, and a tablecloth.

Around 10:00, the whole Hansel clan gathered on the picnic grounds by Ten Mile Lake, staking a claim in the shade by moving wooden picnic tables to the area. Grandma Galena and her sister, Alma; their brothers Roy, Clarence, and Hilmer; and all of their children and grandchildren were the picnic guests. As the families arrived, they set casseroles and roasters, wrapped in newspaper and white flour sack dishtowels, on long wooden picnic tables. Our mouths watered at the aroma of fried chicken, meatballs, ham, baked beans, and scalloped potatoes, while our eyes feasted on potato salads, Jell-O salads in the latest Tupperware containers, watermelon, buttered buns, pickles, and homemade pies. Uncle Roy brought a five-gallon bucket of ice cream wrapped in a green canvas casing. Lillian brought a lemon roll, and Marjorie brought peach pie.

The women wore casual floral dresses that featured a small waist and a full, swinging skirt falling below the knee. The men wore slacks and dress hats, a few boys dared to wear shorts, and we girls received new pedal pusher outfits or we came in a dress.

Horseshoes

After dinner, the men pitched horseshoes as we kids watched. They competed more to outwit each other than to make a ringer, and no one could outdo Dad and his brother Donnie when it came to telling stories, pulling pranks, and kidding each other. Dad said they must first review the rules for Donnie, and he joked that he didn't want Donnie as a partner because he did not release the horseshoe. Donnie said he couldn't have Dad as partner because he was blind.

"I think we should let Donnie stand a few feet closer to the pole so he can compete with us more experienced players," Dad said as he marked a spot a foot away from the post. "Hey, Donnie," Dad teased, "this sport is more fun if you release the horseshoe rather than hold it."

Flailing his arms and shooing us kids away, Donnie said, "Move back, kids. Move way back. In fact, you may want to hide behind a tree. It's Milton's turn to throw, and he doesn't have good aim."

"The point of the game is to get your horseshoe around the post for three points—not to throw it over the post," Dad taunted Donnie.

Meanwhile, the women sat on blankets and took care of babies and toddlers as they exchanged recipes, talked about weddings and showers, and caught up on *Days of Our Lives* and *As the World Turns*. Grandma would tell a funny story from her past and get everyone laughing.

Swimming

An hour after eating, the adults moved to the lake to lifeguard as we kids swam for a couple of hours. Everyone had a wonderful time there. The children splashed and swam, while the teenagers just hung out.

About 5:00 we cleaned the picnic area, leaving no trace of our visit behind, and packed to leave for home. We had barn chores to do, and we looked forward to the sparklers we knew our parents would have for us after it got dark.

He will yet fill your mouth with laughter
and your lips with shouts of joy.
–Job 8:21(NIV)

CHAPTER 24

Halloween

On a cold and windy night, Halloween excitement escalated as we finished our chores, donned our costumes, piled in the car, and headed to Dalton for trick-or-treating. "Watch for witches on brooms and bats gliding above your heads," Dad warned us as he drove. "And don't let moans from behind the trees scare you. It's only ghosts." Mom took a stockpile of candy to Grandma's to hand out to trick-or-treaters, while Dad went along to make sure Grandma's house looked and sounded properly haunted.

Trick-or-treating was safe, lighthearted fun. We knew everyone in Dalton, and the thought would never have crossed our minds that someone would give us an unsafe treat. Halloween was simply a night to have fun and celebrate a rich tradition with the community.

I garnered my Halloween disguises, silly rather than scary, from things in our attic or from Grandma's upstairs storage. One of Grandma's vintage long black dresses, a hat, granny shoes, and a cane transformed me into a whimsical old woman, or one of Grandpa's ratty old shirts, a straw hat, suspenders, and a tie disguised me as a comical old man or an amusing clown. Torn clothes, patched-up bib overalls, a dirt-smudged face, and a bandanna tied to a stick turned me into a destitute hobo.

My imagination played games with me on this night of innocent fun and pranks. Leaves blew everywhere, and moonlight highlighted the outlines of branches so they looked like witches flying. Guided by yard lights, we traveled in packs with friends along ghost-haunted streets as we visited nearly every house in Dalton. Most of the front doors were open and the porch lights lit. When doors opened, we yelled, "Trick or treat!" and held out our brown paper bags. Adults tried to guess who we were before giving us candy or pennies. It was part of their fun. They pretended to be afraid and commented on our costumes. After making our way through town, out of breath, chilled, and with a whole load of candy, we returned to Grandma's house to collapse on her couch. With frozen fingers, we opened our bags to examine our loot.

School Halloween Party

Our school Halloween party was even more exciting than trick-or-treating. Enthusiasm and creative ideas emerged while we planned decorations, food, and games for the annual event. The food committee made witches' brew (which tasted a lot like punch), batty cupcakes, and pumpkin cookies. To decorate the school gymnasium, we constructed ghosts, ghouls, and goblins and hung them from the ceiling lights, propped witches on broomsticks, dangled scary skeletons and formidable bats from the ceiling, and clipped menacing black spiders to creepy fake webs. Jointed black cats with arched backs sat in windows, and carved jack-o-lanterns glowing with candlelight adorned the tables. We draped orange and black twisted crepe paper streamers everywhere and plunked a scarecrow in some cornstalks.

The eighth-graders transformed the school's stage into a haunted house complete with mysterious noises and rattling chains. Each student walked through this dark pathway alone. Skeletons and scary bats dangled from the ceiling. Eighth-graders dressed as ghosts and witches jumped out taunting the thrill-seekers, waving their arms and screaming. A vampire moaned and then someone grabbed our legs. We screamed in delight.

Scavenger Hunt

The game committee at school organized the standard apple bob, musical chairs, and a treasure hunt. Since all the students wanted to participate in the scavenger hunt, our teacher planned the lists. Divided into teams of four or five, we received a list of objects to find around town in one hour. The list included items such as an acorn, apple, bubble gum, candy corn, gopher tail, gourd, Hershey's candy bar, Indian corn, orange leaf, pheasant feather, rickrack, pumpkin seeds, spider web, straw or hay, thread, today's newspaper, Tootsie Rolls, tree bark, and vines. Running all over town, ringing doorbells to ask for items, and searching in dark places for those hard-to-find objects was exhilarating.

This is the day the LORD has made;
let us rejoice and be glad in it.
–Psalm 118:24 (NIV)

Christmas 1951

CHAPTER 25

A Season of Joy and Peace

If I could relive a specific time from my childhood, I would wish for December, any December, because it was a month-long celebration filled with magical and exciting sights, sounds, tastes, and feelings in my mind and heart. It was a time of peace and joy. People wished each other a Merry Christmas, and everyone looked for opportunities to be a light to others, to reach out and serve. Even now, I love how people make a special effort to be kinder, more considerate of others, and more generous during the Christmas season.

Our joy and excitement was encouraged by our parents through traditions of gifts, music, food, decorating, Santa Claus, and family gatherings. Preparation for each activity was as exciting as the celebration itself. Our community embraced the spirit of Christmas through parties, "Saturday with Santa," and a much-loved school Christmas program.

A Spirit of Giving

I fondly remember Christmas being a time of peace on Earth and good will toward others. People seemed especially eager to give to the needy, elderly, and lonely during the holidays. Christmas was a time of helping those less fortunate than ourselves. Parents and teachers brainstormed ideas with us, since even we kids wanted to reach out to those less fortunate in our community. We might brighten an elderly person's life by caroling at her door, bring a handcrafted centerpiece to someone sick, or deliver a fruit basket to a family with little to eat.

Mom baked cookies for the bachelor farmer, we kids visited an old woman who lived alone, Dad delivered meat to a needy family, Grandma baked for the shut-ins in town, and we delivered a box of apples to a less-fortunate neighbor. We also spread cheer through the exchange of holiday cards.

We were made to believe that a homemade gift was far superior to a gift bought in a store. Therefore, every year I embroidered, knit, and crafted Christmas gifts. One year I purchased yarn at the general store and knit slippers with pompons for family members. Grandma taught me how to crochet circular potholders; and for the younger kids she made stuffed monkeys out of men's brown-and-white work socks that had a distinctive red, crescent heel, which was used for the face.

Other years, we gave inexpensive "store-bought" presents. We kids saved a portion of our allowance all year to be able to bestow small gifts on one another. On a night while staying with Grandma, I trekked to the hardware store to purchase dollar Christmas gifts. Meandering the crowded aisles towering with housewares, toys, tools, paint, and hardware, I selected a paint-by-number set for Audrey, a model car kit for Warren, Old Maid cards for Jo, and a Roy Rogers gun and holster set for Daryl. I purchased Old Spice aftershave for Dad, a blue bottle of Evening in Paris cologne for Mom, and a pack of three embroidered handkerchiefs for Grandma.

This anticipation of Christmas began weeks before December 25 for our parents as they budgeted to sell a pig or a load of wheat to make Christmas extra special for us kids.

Christmas Cards

Mom was a dedicated sender of Christmas cards because, as she said, she didn't want to miss the opportunity to touch base with friends and family, especially her relatives in North Dakota. Christmas cards to family members in North Dakota included a letter, since this was a time when long-distance phone calls were expensive. Christmas cards were exchanged with friends and neighbors in the community, and we delighted over the beautiful cards we received in the mail each day.

Christmas Dresses

I have fond memories of the Christmas dresses Grandma made for us girls. This was our one new dress each year, and we wore it to all of the holiday events. Sometimes Grandma made jumpers paired with crisp white blouses, or pleated skirts with blouses that each had a Peter Pan collar. One year the dress she made had short puffy sleeves and a full skirt of shimmery chiffon. We were always so proud of our beautiful dresses.

Dress fittings were a special time with Grandma. I remember the gentle feel of her trying the ecru tissue paper pattern pieces on us for the right fit. With the tape measure draped around her neck, she pinned each pattern piece to the fabric. Soon we heard the snip of scissors crunch their way through the layers. Threads littered the floor, and we heard another whoosh as the hot iron pressed damp cloths down on a newly sewn seam.

Finally, Grandma would make us stand on a chair so she could check the hems and seam. We were very proud to wear our Christmas dresses that Grandma lovingly made each year. Dad would always say, "You girls sure look spiffy."

Santa Claus

My active imagination allowed me to believe in many things that added adventure and excitement to my life. I accepted the Easter bunny, tooth fairy, baby stork, Norwegian elves, and other mythical entities intangible to me. Therefore, I also believed in Santa Claus who lived at the North Pole with his elves and reindeer. I fully trusted that reindeer flew and Santa traveled to children all over the world on one night.

I am thankful that our community and family embraced the Santa Claus myth because it laid the foundation for what it means to give and receive. At our house, Santa was someone who loved children and brought us each one gift.

Our belief in Santa Claus did not conflict with our belief in Jesus. We knew Christmas was the day we celebrated the birth of Jesus. The holiday also taught us values such as generosity, kindness, and goodwill toward others.

When the Sears Roebuck and Montgomery Ward *Wish Books* arrived, we kids began formulating our letters to Santa. We knew to ask Santa for only one thing. We girls requested a doll, doctor kit, Nancy Drew mystery book, or Easy Sewing cards. Daryl asked for a Tonka farm machine, Lincoln Logs, or Tinker Toys, and Warren asked for a chemistry set or microscope. The little kids asked for a jack-in-the-box, spinning top, wooden building blocks, wind-up animals, Fisher-Price Tuggy Turtle, or a Huffy Puffy Train.

When we reached the point where we began to question the fantasy of Santa Claus, we never discussed it—Mom cautioned us that only believers received gifts from Santa. This wonderful belief in Santa was a well-guarded secret. Not one of us older kids would dare destroy that magical way of thinking for our younger siblings. We competed with Dad in most creatively embellishing Santa fabrications for our brothers and sisters, and we delighted in watching the joy on their faces when they discovered what Santa had brought for them.

Make a Joyful Noise

Music played a significant part in setting the mood for Christmas. Within the confines of our family, no one was self-conscious about their singing voice. At home, Mom loved music the most. In the kitchen, Christmas carols rang out from the radio as she sang along with Frank Sinatra to "Have Yourself a Merry Little Christmas," Bing Crosby to "White Christmas," Andy Williams to "It's the Most Wonderful Time of the Year," and Dean Martin to "Let it Snow! Let it Snow! Let it Snow!" We kids learned all the lyrics to "It's Beginning to Look a Lot Like Christmas," "I Saw Mommy Kissing Santa Claus," and "How Much Is That Doggie in the Window." From the barn radio, we sang along to "Blue Christmas" by Elvis Presley, "I Just Go Nuts at Christmas," and "Jingle Bells."

While listening to Gene Autry's album on the old console stereo, we memorized all the verses to "Rudolph the Red-Nosed Reindeer," "Up On the Housetop," "Here Comes Santa Claus," and "Frosty the Snowman." We listened to Burl Ives sing "Have a Holly Jolly Christmas," and we danced as Brenda Lee sang "Rockin' Around the Christmas Tree." On our large upright piano, we girls rattled out tunes as we belted out the words to "It Came Upon a Midnight Clear." We taught the little ones to sing "All I Want for Christmas Is My Two Front Teeth," "I'm Gettin' Nuttin' for Christmas," "We Wish You a Merry Christmas," "I Want a Hippopotamus for Christmas," and "Santa Claus Is Coming to Town."

In school, the religious and the secular—Jesus and Santa—were intermixed in the Christmas program. We absorbed the true meaning of Christmas through music. By singing and listening to Christmas carols, we learned great theology and heard about the true meaning of Christmas.

"Silent Night," "Away in a Manger," and "O Little Town of Bethlehem" helped make Christmas a celebration of Jesus's birth. "Angels We Have Heard on High," "Joy to the World," "We Three Kings," and "Hark! The Herald Angels Sing" taught us the story of Mary, Joseph, and the baby Jesus. "The First Noel," "While Shepherds Watched Their Flocks by Night," and "O Come, All Ye Faithful" added to the celebration of this wonderful holiday.

Holiday Baking

We baked all year, but at Christmas we used our special holiday recipes. Some family favorites were Russian tea cookies, date balls, and no-bake chocolate cookies. Mom quickly mastered the skill of Norwegian holiday baking. She taught us girls how to make krumkake, sandbakkels, rosettes, spritz cookies, and lefse. These specialties were holiday treats, and we would never dream of making them any other time of the year.

Krumkake, a delicate cone-shaped butter cookie, is baked between two flat irons on the stovetop. Pouring batter on the hot iron, we squeezed the irons together, baking it first on one side, then the other. Removing the now-baked dough, we shaped it around a wooden cone. To make rosettes, we dipped a snowflake-shaped iron into batter and then into boiling lard. As these crisp lacy pastries cooled on brown paper, we sprinkled them with sugar. We pressed sugar cookie dough into small fluted pans to make sandbakkels.

We girls loved to make butter and sugar spritz cookies because there were so many variations. We added green food coloring to the dough to make trees, red food coloring for the stockings, and left them white for snowmen. We substituted almond for vanilla, or we made the batter chocolate. We pushed stiff dough into the spritz tube and twisted the handle to make shapes on the cookie sheet, or we placed discs shaped like a tree, star, or wreath in the end of the cookie press to create different shapes. Then we sprinkled the cookies with edible glitter before baking them.

Rolling out white sugar dough, we cut them with metal cookie cutters in the shape of stars, trees, angels, and bells. Before we popped them in the oven, we covered them with red or green sprinkles and silver beads. We also made divinity, fudge, and popcorn balls.

Dad indulged us with store-bought candy that was shaped like a ribbon, peanut brittle, large cream drops with a chocolate coating, chocolate-covered cherries, Red Delicious apples, and hard candy of different shapes and sizes—sometimes with a chewy center. On the kitchen table, a wooden bowl with a holder in the middle for a metal nutcracker and picks brimmed over with walnuts, almonds, hazelnuts, peanuts, pecans, and Brazil nuts.

At Grandma's house a pleasant spicy *sot suppe* (sweet soup) made with raisins, prunes, apricots, cinnamon, sugar, and tapioca would be simmering on the stove. I helped her make *fattigmann*, deep-fried cookies flavored with cardamom and sprinkled with sugar. For an entire month, we kids would ravage through the tins and boxes of homemade cookies Grandma stored on the cool steps leading to her unused upstairs.

Grandma rolled out and fried *flatbrød* (flat bread), and she also made *rømmergrøt*, a porridge made with cream, butter, and flour. She said she made it because it brought back childhood memories. The secret to liking it, Grandma said, was to add lots of cream, cinnamon, and sugar.

Lefse

Making lefse, a much-loved Christmas tradition in our family, required special vintage equipment. On the December day reserved for lefse-making, Dad drove to town to collect Grandma, who assisted Mom with the daylong mission. In advance, Mom peeled and boiled thirty pounds of potatoes and cleaned the black wood-burning stovetop.

The process went like clockwork for Grandma and Mom. White potatoes, mashed with butter and heavy farm cream, were strained through a metal ricer to remove any lumps. Adding flour, sugar, and salt, Mom formed the mixture into egg-sized balls ready for rolling.

Sprinkling a hefty handful of flour on the kitchen table, Grandma flattened a ball with her hand, turned it over in the flour, selected the first of three rolling pins, and began to roll the lefse until it was very thin. From the center, she rolled the lefse outward, and with each stroke she rotated the direction so the dough formed into a round shape. To avoid sticking, Grandma dusted a little more flour on the board and continued with a light rolling touch.

After Grandma rolled the dough to perfection, Mom rolled it onto a long, flat lefse stick and unrolled it on the black stovetop to bake. When brown spots appeared, she flipped it to bake on the other side, bursting any air bubbles with a lefse stick. She removed it from stove, stacked it in a crisp clean dishtowel, brushed the flour off the stove, and started with the next piece of lefse.

"*Denne lefse lukter godt*! (This lefse smells good!)" Dad said as he walked through the door, stomping snow off his four bucklers at noon and grinning at the exhausted women. We kids anxiously anticipated getting home from school to taste the warm, delicious lefse.

Shiny Bright Ornaments and Silver Tinsel

We always had a real Christmas tree. After examining the trees on the lot in Dalton, we selected a large, tall pine for our house and another one for Grandma. The tree reigned as the focal point of our Christmas decorating and gave our home a pleasant pine scent. After sawing off the right amount from the tree's base, Dad anchored it in a sizeable metal stand and secured it with metal screws.

Warren retrieved our Christmas trimmings from the attic. The tree lights went on first; they were larger than most of them are today. They were painted blue, green, red, orange, and yellow, with the colors alternating throughout the string. We tested the lights before Dad hung them, knowing that a single burned-out bulb would case them all to quit working. A white dishtowel served as a tree skirt.

The ornaments—glass balls—went on next. Although everyone participated in decorating the tree, only Mom handled the fragile glass ornaments. We watched as she removed bells and ornaments from the sectioned ornament boxes and placed them lovingly on the tree. When she was finished, we draped silver tinsel on the branches. Each of us kids would receive a handful, and we were instructed to drape one strand at a time onto the branches. The final touch was adding the silver glass spire that topped our tree year after year.

I loved basking in the glow of the tree lights after we switched the main lights off. By morning, a makeshift fence of chairs surrounded the tree to keep away toddlers. Motorists traveling on the road observed red bells gracing our front bay window.

Bunco

The 4-H Christmas Bunco party, held on a Saturday night in December, was a social highlight of the season. The evening was a dressy affair, and I loved wearing my new Christmas dress that Grandma made for me. Entering our school gymnasium, we each received a tally card directing us to our respective tables. As I glanced around at twenty card tables covered with dice, score pads, and pencils, I found my spot and sat across from my partner. The other two people at the table were my opponents.

Someone at the head table shouted, "Go!" Dice instantaneously hit the tables while shouts of encouragement grew louder. It was hard to hear above the roar of yelling and laughter. Arms flailed upward, and people shouted, but Dad's laugh rose above all the noise.

My turn came to role three dice. I needed ones. I rolled a one, so I rolled the dice again. I got two ones, so I shook again, adding my points. This time I shook three twos.

"Bunco!" I screamed.

"Sorry, that's worth five points. You need three ones for bunco this round," said an adult at the table.

When I quit getting ones, I passed the dice to my opponent, who shook three ones.

"Bunco!" she yelled as she threw three ones and received twenty-one points.

After six rounds, the other team held the highest score, giving them the privilege of moving ahead a table, while we all received a new partner before moving on to the next round. Between sets, we laughed and talked until we heard someone shout, "Go!"

After many rounds, prizes were awarded to the high and low scorers, followed by lunch and visiting. Before we left, Mom cleaned the kitchen, and Dad locked up the school.

Saturday with Santa

I remember as a child how festive our little village seemed during December. Huge red bells and wreaths hung on long strings of giant green garland across Dalton's Main Street, and familiar carols resonated from loudspeakers. A tall gaily-decorated Christmas tree graced a four-way intersection. The air was filled with an aura of something much bigger. To me, it was the perfect world of smiling familiar faces, people cheerfully stopping to talk, and a radiant sparkle of Christmas everywhere.

Dalton merchants hosted "Saturday with Santa," which included a movie and a visit from St. Nick. A long rectangular hall with an electric projector placed on a raised platform served as the town theatre. The movie always stopped midway so the reels could be changed. As the picture ended, Santa arrived to deliver a gift to each child. Shopkeepers gave away potholders, glass bowls, or calendars to the adults.

Handcrafted Ornaments

In school, each classroom had a real Christmas tree, and we kids decorated them with handcrafted ornaments. Limited only by our imaginations, we worked with items readily available such as pinecones, berries, large seedpods, cinnamon sticks, old Christmas cards, and rickrack. The teachers provided a few craft embellishments such as glue, glitter, gems, sequins, felt, pipe cleaners, tinfoil, construction paper, ribbons, yarn, tinsel, cotton balls, and cans of spray paint.

We painted milkweed pods and sprinkled them with glitter, decorated miniature pinecone trees, and constructed wreaths from various trimmings. We used a cookie cutter to create paper gingerbread men and glued on decorations, and we made snowmen out of Styrofoam balls. Adding pipe cleaners for antlers, a miniature red pompom for the nose, and glued-on eyes, we turned candy canes into reindeer. We also made reindeer out of clothespins with little red fuzz balls glued on for noses.

Deck the Halls

We created snowflakes by folding the paper into eighths and cutting triangles or fancy designs, and then we hung them in the window for everyone to see. The walls were decorated with construction-paper Santas adorned with cotton ball beards and green construction-paper trees covered in glitter. The better artists made chalk drawings on the blackboards, and the rest of us made green and red paper chains to drape around the room.

Homemade Christmas Gifts

With great secrecy, we made presents for our parents. In the younger grades, we formed plaster handprints and sat for silhouettes. We glued the previous year's Christmas cards to empty three-gallon cardboard ice cream containers to make wastebaskets, or stuck uncooked macaroni onto empty soup cans and spray-painted them gold to make pencil holders. With Popsicle sticks, we made trivets.

We glued pictures from old Christmas cards on jar lids and added glitter, rickrack, felt, ribbon, and yarn. Potholders were made from looped material that we wove back and forth on a small metal frame with prongs to hold the looped ends.

In seventh grade, we made beautiful wax candles using school milk cartons, paraffin wax, and old crayons. We tied string to a pencil and laid it across the milk carton for the wick. After we melted the paraffin, we added pieces of crayon and poured the mixture into the milk carton. When the candle set, we took off the milk carton and decorated the outside of the candle. We made Christmas cards to bring along and give to seniors when we went caroling.

Caroling

"Spreading joy," as our teachers called it, was an opportunity for farm kids to spend an evening in town as we caroled, singing "*Jeg Er Så Glad*" ("I Am So Glad"), "Silent Night," "The First Noel," and "O Little Town of Bethlehem." I relished the crisp evening air and the glow of lights as we walked through town, going from house to house singing beloved Christmas songs. We went to homes of seniors and gave them each a small gift or ornament we had made in the classroom. Without a doubt, this meant even more to us than it did to them.

Gift Exchange

On the last day of school before the Christmas break, we had a Christmas party. Planning the classroom party was as much fun as attending it. Kids could be on the decoration committee, food committee, gift exchange committee, or game committee. I always chose the food committee because I could share our Christmas baking.

We had a gift exchange with a fifty-cent limit. We gave each other gifts such as books of Life Saver candies and bath beads. Teachers gave us pencils with our names on them, and we often gave our teachers a beautiful embroidered handkerchief.

School Christmas Program

The annual all-school Christmas program was one of the most exciting events of the year, not only for the students and teachers but also for the whole community. We kids were excited about performing for our families and all the other guests. What we lacked in musical ability we made up for in enthusiasm. I remember the faces of parents, grandparents, aunts, uncles, and cousins as we sang "Silent Night," "Away in a Manger," "Hark! The Herald Angels Sing," "Gloria," and other songs of celebration and worship.

The teachers each selected a humorous Christmas play that went along the personality of their classroom. When we returned from Thanksgiving vacation, students were assigned various parts, with each child getting a role to play. Miss Moen sent us home clutching mimeographed scripts with red underlined parts to memorize. She also picked time-honored Christmas carols for us to sing.

Rehearsal at school occupied our afternoons, and at home we older kids practiced our parts in front of Mom's vanity and helped our younger siblings memorize their lines. Teachers worried about students not memorizing their roles and not talking loud enough, both of which I excelled at.

When the big night arrived, we entered the school decked out in new Christmas outfits and darted up the stairs to our classrooms; while our parents, grandparents, and other community members greeted neighbors and friends in the gymnasium. As the room got more crowded, men gave women their seats and stood at the back. Excitement grew as the crowd waited, hoping their children would remember their lines.

Promptly at 8:00 p.m. (it was late, but this was a farming community and farmers had to finish milking), Miss Moen played soft music on the piano, inviting the audience to stop talking. Curtains opened to the nervous faces of first- and second-graders, each holding a large red alphabet letter spelling out Merry Christmas. Each child recited a two-line verse as he or she held up their card. "C is for Christmas, our favorite time of year," "H is for houses, decorated merry and bright." The hushed audience listened with rapt attention. Teachers held scripts ready to prompt anyone who needed it. A few of the kids always forgot their lines. I beamed as my sister remembered what to say even as she twirled the skirt on her dress and shaded her eyes trying to find Mom and Dad in the audience.

Next, the children used rhythm sticks, tambourines, and bells as they sang "Rudolph the Red-Nosed Reindeer" and "Jingle Bells." Marching off stage, they waved to their parents and then sat down in front-row reserved seats. The audience eagerly applauded. The intermediate class presented a heartwarming Christmas play and sang "Silent Night" and "Joy to the World." The upper grade presented a humorous play and sang "It Came Upon a Midnight Clear" and "O Little Town of Bethlehem." For a finale, all three classes assembled on stage to sing "We Wish You a Merry Christmas."

The adults got a chance to perform as well. To end the special evening, the audience stood and sang the Norwegian Christmas song "*Jeg Er Så Glad*" ("I Am So Glad"):

> *Jeg er så glad hver julekveld,*
> *for da ble Jesus født,*
> *da lyste stjernen som en sol,*
> *og engler sang så søtt.*

(I am so glad each Christmas Eve,
for when Jesus was born,
when the star shone like the sun,
and the angels sang.)

I first became aware of the power of Christmas carols to move an audience as I stood on the stage and watched the tearful audience sing this happy song.

When the song ended, Santa Claus arrived with a jingling of sleigh bells and a merry "Ho! Ho! Ho!" He opened his sack and delivered little paper bags of Christmas goodies—an apple, peanuts, and hard Christmas candy—to every child in the room. My parents lingered to visit, and Dad helped put away folding chairs, started the engines on teachers' cars, and locked the school before we piled into our car and headed home.

Our parents affirmed that we were the best actors they had ever seen and the entire performance was a work of genius. We were stars in their eyes.

Elated, I could hear the wind whistling through the cracks in the house as I snuggled under my big quilts. The house got quieter as everyone settled down to sleep, comforted by the joy and wonder of Christmas. It was on these nights I had trouble falling asleep as I relived the magical evening and savored the excitement of the Christmas season.

"Glory to God in the highest,
and on earth peace to men on whom his favor rests."
–Luke 2:14 (NIV)

Christmas 1952

CHAPTER 26

Christmas on the Farm

In addition to the fun we had at school and in town, we also enjoyed family Christmas traditions on the farm. Waiting for Santa, exchanging gifts, attending Midnight Mass, and spending time with relatives were always highlights of the holiday season.

The Magic of Santa

Our parents explained how Santa could get into every house in one night, and we believed them. After all, Christmas was magical. We kids were giddy the entire morning and afternoon of December 24 because we knew Santa would soon be delivering gifts to us. Somehow he knew that our family celebrated Christmas on Christmas Eve.

Almost every year, Dad and my little brother, Daryl, saw reindeer and sleigh tracks in the snow. Dad loved to play with our innocent imaginations through a bit of deception, and Daryl desperately wanted to believe him—so much so that he convinced himself that he'd witnessed the reindeer with his own eyes. Of course Dad helped by putting sleigh tracks in the snow and setting out hay and carrots, which disappeared after the Santa "sighting."

"Oh, my gosh!" Dad said as he bounded inside with Daryl tagging along. "Working out in the barn I heard sleigh bells, so I dropped the pitchfork, hollered for Daryl, and ran outside. Lo and behold, Santa and his reindeer were up on the barn roof!"

"Did you see them, Daryl?" I asked.

Daryl tipped back on his heels and took a deep breath, "Yep, I saw them."

"I didn't see Rudolph leading the sleigh. Did you see him, Daryl?" Dad asked.

"No, I don't think so," Daryl replied.

"Dad, Rudolph only travels when it's foggy," Jo explained.

"Well, anyway, I caught a glimpse of eight reindeer and Santa with a sleigh load of toys," Dad assured us.

"I heard a noise," Mom said as she entered the kitchen. "Were you kids playing in the living room?"

We abandoned our game and darted to the living room, which quickly echoed with wild shouts of excitement. "Santa has been here!" we yelled.

"Hurry!" Dad hollered. "He's just leaving—he's on the roof!" We'd rush out and try to catch a glimpse of Santa Claus, but we never did see him.

We each received one gift from Santa, which we were allowed to open after the Christmas Eve dinner. Apparently, we all forgot what we had asked for—we tried to guess the contents of our present based on how the box rattled and how much it weighed. Dad became like a child again as he crawled under the tree to examine the gifts. "I wonder what this is," he said as he rattled a box.

The Nisse

Christmas Eve seemed like the longest day of the year. Minutes passed like hours, since our festivities could not begin until Dad returned from finishing his barn chores.

"Well, I took care of Nils," Dad said as he stomped snow off his boots and shut the door. "I fed the livestock an extra ration of hay and oats and left hot cream with lots of butter for the nisse (this is what Dad called the little Norwegian elf who supposedly lived in our barn)."

"Why?" asked one of the little kids.

"Man, two years ago, I forgot to feed the cattle an extra ration on Christmas Eve, and the mischievous nisse got angry at me and made a mess in the barn."

"Is Nils a bad elf?"

"No," said Dad. "But if you don't take good care of the animals, he will cause trouble for you. He is insistent that all animals get an extra portion of food on Christmas Eve."

"What kind of trouble does he cause?" asked a little one.

"The year I forgot to give the cattle their extra ration, Nils unscrewed all the light bulbs in the barn and opened all the stanchions. When I went to the barn on Christmas morning, the cattle were wandering all over. What a mess that was!"

Christmas Eve Celebration

Chores were done early on Christmas Eve so the festivities could begin. When Dad finally washed and changed into clean clothes, we began our celebration. It started with our traditional

Christmas Eve dinner. Dad, Grandma, and we kids took our places at the dining room table. Mom set the platter of lutefisk, dripping with melted butter, between Grandma and Dad. Oven-baked Swiss steak, gravy, mashed potatoes, scalloped corn, salad, chocolate chip dessert, and lefse rolled with butter and brown sugar completed our meal. We all felt happy and contented since we were with the family we loved.

After supper (even before dishes), we moved to the living room to open gifts. "I'm passing out the gifts," Warren announced as he started to sort the presents into piles.

"Be careful with the paper so we can use it again next year," Mom told him.

"I don't know, maybe we should wait until morning," Dad teasingly contemplated.

"No!" we all shouted.

"Okay, I guess you can pass out the gifts, Warren," Dad said, chuckling.

Chaos ensued as everyone tore open their gifts, leaving wrapping paper strewn across the living room. We kids opened Santa's gifts first. Audrey's Chatty Cathy doll talked when you pulled on her string. Jo received a doll with blinking eyes. I cherished a musical jewelry box with a tiny ballerina figurine. Warren got a chemistry set, and the little boys got toy tractors.

It didn't really matter to me what appeared below the Christmas tree. The excitement of watching others open the gifts I had made for them was a thrill for me.

"Wow, you made this!" Mom said as she opened an unrecognizable lump of clay with handprints on it.

"I can't believe you bought me handkerchiefs," Dad said. "That is exactly what I wanted."

Grandma's gifts were handmade: rag dolls, doll clothes, or

doll blankets for us girls, and a new pair of homemade flannel pajamas for each child. Grandma gave Mom a set of embroidered days-of-the-week dishtowels. Dad and Mom said their biggest present was seeing the smiles on the faces of their children.

With all the gifts opened, Mom and Grandma headed to the kitchen to do dishes, while Dad assembled a toy highchair for one of my little sisters. This was the one night of the year Mom would not allow us girls to do dishes. She said it was a night for children to play and enjoy themselves.

Baby Jesus in a Manger

"Kids, be sure you have your gloves and scarves; and Maxine, grab a blanket," Mom said. "It's brutally cold outside."

The cold weather did not deter Mom from her Midnight Mass pilgrimage each year. Around 11:00 on Christmas Eve, Mom and the older kids piled into the Chevy and headed to Fergus Falls while Dad stayed home with the little ones. Freezing temperatures, blowing and drifting snow, and the midnight hour were of no concern to Mom because, as she said more than once, "Jesus' birthday is the reason we celebrate Christmas." Midnight Mass connected her to the real meaning of Christmas, and it was the lone Christmas tradition from her childhood that she retained in her new community.

We crowded shoulder-to-shoulder in the pews to sing "Silent Night" and "It Came Upon a Midnight Clear." Shadows from candlelight danced against the walls, and scarlet poinsettias lined the altar. The solemn serenity of the night made it impossible not to sense the real meaning of Christmas. Sitting there in the achingly beautiful candlelight service, the truth and purpose of this season began to settle into my bones.

When we left church, snow was falling. Mom drove home

on icy roads with sleeping kids in the car. As I opened my eyes to see wind whipping snow across the road, I noticed Mom yawn. "Mom, how did you celebrate Christmas when you were a kid?" I asked.

"Our Christmas was blessed by traditions I hold close to my heart. We fasted on Christmas Eve, eating only fish and raisin bread, and we hung our stockings on a clothesline strung across the kitchen. The memory I cherish the most was my Mom and Dad waking us up before midnight to ride in the sleigh to Midnight Mass. Christmas morning, Dad and Mom lit the candles on our tree, and we opened our presents from Santa. It was special."

Christmas Day Family Gathering

The farm was everyone's Bethlehem, the place that Grandma, parents, aunts, uncles, cousins, and siblings were drawn to at Christmas, the place they called home. Dad's brothers and their families traveled quite a distance to spend Christmas Day on the farm. Sharing memories going decades back always prompted both laughter and tears. Christmas was a day of feasting, nostalgia, love, laughter, and making new memories.

We girls helped Mom prepare a feast of ham, mashed potatoes, gravy, scalloped corn, sweet potatoes, coleslaw, lime Jell-o, and blueberry dessert. We peeled two mammoth kettles of potatoes, chopped cabbage, cut celery, whipped cream, peeled carrots, cut pickles, spread butter and brown sugar on the lefse, and set the dining room and kitchen tables with our best china and silverware. We delighted in making a special Christmas punch by mixing red powder, sugar, and ginger ale.

When it was time to eat, Dad sliced the ham, Mom made gravy, and I mashed the potatoes with a wood-handled potato masher. We kids ate around the big kitchen table while adults ate in the dining room and embarked upon a sentimental journey of Christmases past. Merriment was contagious.

After the dishes were done, we kids spent the day outdoors sledding, ice skating, and playing King of the Hill with our cousins. At dusk, we headed for the house, hungry and happy. We came inside with snow caked to our snow pants, mittens, and jackets, our toes and fingers numb and nearly frozen, and our noses dripping.

The women set out a smorgasbord of leftovers from dinner, and we piled our plates for the second time that day. After the china and silver were washed and put away, the relatives began to leave, encouraged by Dad to take a package of steaks or a roast, along with a pound of butter. Finally, Dad and a couple of us kids headed to the barn. Even on Christmas, the cows needed to be milked.

Julebrukers

We anticipated Julebrukers one of the nights between Christmas and New Year's Eve. It started with car horns honking, people boisterously hitting on kettles, and shouts of "Yulabrook." Revelers knocked at the door and rushed inside when Dad opened it. Disguised with paper bags, nylon stockings, or masks on their heads, and dressed in hobo-type clothes, they danced around the kitchen, waved at us, and made silly gestures. Mom and Dad knew the revelers would not say anything or remove their masks until we guessed the person behind the mask. After much laughter and guessing, their identities were revealed. They guzzled a drink and then left for their next stop. Dad laughed and told us stories of his younger years when he had been one of the masquerading Julebrukers.

The Year Mom Spent Christmas in the Hospital

One Christmas memory stands out from all the others. Christmas Eve 1957 began the same as all other Christmas Eves. Everyone was busy, and Mom was working to make Christmas special for her family: wrapping gifts, baking Christmas treats, and cooking. We did not notice how sick Mom was because, after all, it was Christmas Eve and we were too excited about Santa coming. She made our usual Christmas dinner. As we finished opening our presents, I heard Dad say, "I'm taking Mom to the hospital. She's sick. You girls take care of the dishes and the kids."

"Aren't we going to midnight mass?"

"No, your mother is sick," Dad said. "Warren, if I'm not back by morning, you can start milking."

We cleared the table, washed the dishes, and got all the younger ones to bed. Little did we know that Mom would spend the next seven days in the hospital due to a punctured eardrum. I had turned eleven earlier that year and was used to doing most of the household chores. As the oldest girl, I became the one in charge. It fell to Audrey, Jo, and me to prepare the meals, watch the little ones, keep the house clean, and wash and iron the clothes. Only five months old, our sister Eydie needed to be fed, diapered, and bathed, while three-year-old Daryl entertained himself with his toy tractors. Neighbors stopped by with food and goodies and never left without praising us for being so mature.

She will give birth to a son, and you are to give him the name Jesus,
because he will save his people from their sins.
–Matthew 1:21 (NIV)

Christmas 1954

Christmas 1955

Christmas 1957

Christmas 1958

PART SEVEN

Community

CHAPTER 27

Visiting

Our community valued hospitality and relationships, and our lives were filled with a bounty of extended family and neighbors. "Dropping in" unannounced showed one's desire to be neighborly, and visitors received a warm welcome along with hot coffee and homemade cookies.

Every day, unexpected company dropped by the farm to chat over a cup of coffee. No matter how busy they were, Mom and Dad stopped whatever they were doing and visited with whomever came by—the man delivering the Sunday morning newspaper, a relative who was in the area, farmers stopping by to ask Dad's advice, a salesperson delivering seed corn, the man filling up the tractor gas barrel, or friends just popping in to say hello. "Don't be a stranger—drop by anytime," visitors always heard when they left.

Our family maintained a strong sense of public connectedness, partly because Grandma and Grandpa's brothers and sisters and their children comprised a big part of the community—many of them owned local businesses and neighboring farms. We celebrated holidays, weddings, birthdays, reunions, graduations, and anniversaries with our Hansel and Bergerson relatives.

Visiting Neighbors

Friday nights and Sunday afternoons were generally the times when we visited neighbors or they visited us. On Friday nights while adults played whist, we kids entertained ourselves outside under the yard light; or, if it was winter, played games upstairs. Around midnight, as the adults laughed and talked while munching on sandwiches, dessert, and coffee, we kids fell asleep on the coats that had been thrown across a bed. Soon, our folks woke us and ushered us to the cold backseat where we snuggled together for warmth as Dad drove home, singing lyrics from a favorite old song: *"Show me the way to go home. I'm tired and I want to go to bed. I had a little drink about an hour ago, and it went right to my head."*

Regular rounds of unannounced visits between families occupied our Sunday afternoons. When the get-together was at our house, we brought our friends to the haymow to dare them to swing across and fall into the hay below. The haymow provided wonderful tunnels, caves, and corners for games of hide-and-seek.

It was expected that the visiting party would stay for Sunday evening supper, but the invite always went something like this:

"You'll stay for supper, of course," Dad said.

"No, we better not," they replied.

"It's barbeques and rice salad—nothing special," Mom chimed in.

"Oh, no, we don't want to inconvenience you."

"It's no trouble. Of course you'll stay," Dad insisted.

"Well, okay, I guess we will, if you're sure."

Our parents considered our public behavior important. Specifically, we knew to stay clear of the adult room, never take a second treat when offered one, say "thank you," and volunteer to wash the dishes.

Sunday Drives

On a rare summer Sunday afternoon, if we did not have visitors or intend to visit anyone, we might ride around in the car with Dad and Mom, watching the fields through the open windows. We took turns sitting by the window to let the breeze blow through our hair as we dangled our hand outside and practiced the hand turn signals for cars. Sometimes, as we were riding along, Dad would reach in the cubbyhole and bring out a bag of circus peanuts to share. When we were older, Mom and Dad might drive us to Fergus Falls to go bowling, attend a movie, or roller skate at the indoor rink.

Whist Card Parties

Everyone in the community with a healthy dose of sarcasm and a great sense of humor played whist. In fact, everyone I knew played whist. During adult card parties, hearty laughter filled our home as friends teased and insulted each other. The boisterous laughter of the adults seemed to shake the walls in the house, everyone trying to talk louder than the next one.

Farm Auctions

Farm auctions were community events that also served as a time to greet old friends. In fact, it would have been downright

un-neighborly not to attend. As Dad said when he came home with
something Mom did not think we needed: "The only neighborly
thing to do is buy something." If it was not a school day, Dad let one
or two of us kids tag along. There was usually a table with coffee
and cookies run by the Ladies Aid.

Cars and pickups lined the long farm driveway and parked
in the fields. People milled around talking and drinking cups of hot
coffee. Tractors, farm machinery, and sometimes livestock headed
the auction bill, followed by tools and miscellaneous farm items,
and finally household goods placed together in boxes on a hayrack
or on tables from the legion. Dad acquired several pieces of farm
equipment at auction sales. Several of our bedroom sets were also
purchased at auction.

Perhaps the most memorable of Dad's purchases was an
old upright piano. Dad thought it would be good to make pianists
of his daughters. The piano remained in our house's east room in
the winter, which we closed off to save money on heat; so we practiced while wearing our coats and hats.

Birthday Parties

Birthday parties were special. The boys invited the boys
in their schoolroom, and the girls invited the girls. Invitations were
handed out at school, and nobody of the same sex was excluded.
Usually the party started after the end of the school day and was
held in our homes. We played party games, opened gifts, sang
"Happy Birthday," blew out candles, and ate birthday cake. The
parents of the birthday person drove each guest home.

Funerals

It was tradition to call on neighbors and relatives who had a death in the family and bring them a hotdish, freshly baked bread, pie, or cake with your name written on the bottom of the pan. I went to many Lutheran funerals. The town stores closed during a funeral because everyone attended. Dad wore his suit, while Mom and Grandma dressed in black dresses, hats, and gloves. Of course, we kids wore our one good church outfit. If it was summer, gladioli were the flowers on the altar. The deceased lay in a casket at the back of the church.

We sang "How Great Thou Art" and "The Old Rugged Cross" at the Norwegian Lutheran funerals in Dalton. After the graveyard service, we went to the church basement to eat hotdish, salad, buns, pickles, cake, and coffee. Mom and Grandma served at many funerals. Grandma buttered the buns. Mom washed the aluminum cake pans and casseroles, setting them on the counter for their owners to retrieve, checking for the family name marked on the bottom of each pan.

Dad's way of dealing with death (as with most difficult situations) was through humor, and the conversation after a funeral usually went something like this:

"He certainly was well liked, judging by the number of people at his funeral. The church was packed," Mom said as we drove home.

"Well, I thought he was an old battle axe," Dad kidded. "All those people came because they wanted a free lunch."

"Oh, Milton, don't say things like that in front of the kids."

"After listening to the soloist, I thought there would be a few more deaths," joked Dad.

"Now, that is enough. You know kids repeat everything."

Weddings

Living in a small, close-knit community, weddings and showers were social events attended by everyone who wanted to come, and almost every woman in the community came. Two weeks prior to the wedding, a sign in the General Store invited all the women and girls in the community to attend a miscellaneous shower for the bride-to-be in the church basement. Most of the community women arrived with sheets, embroidered pillowcases or dishtowels, or other household items the bride would need to start her married life. The program in the church basement consisted of a reading, piano selection, and a solo by a relative. It ended with the traditional lunch of three-layer sandwiches, nuts, mints, cake, and punch.

Weddings commenced at 8:00 p.m. so the farmers could finish milking beforehand. The organist played the wedding march as the bride, wearing a gorgeous white dress, walked down the aisle on her father's arm. A reception followed in the church basement, which was decorated with crepe paper streamers.

The tea-length wedding dress was popular in the 1950s and into the 1960s. Most wedding dresses had a full skirt and were decorated with faux pearls and sequins. Sleeves were long or short, but fitted. Silk and satin were used for the skirt and often taffeta for the bodice. The culture of the time required one to choose cream, antique ivory satin, or off-white if the bride was pregnant.

Shivaree

A shivaree, or noisy serenade, was a continuation of the marriage celebration. The shivaree took place on the Friday or Saturday night following the wedding. Everyone would assemble with something for making noise, such as a metal dishpan or a pot and wooden spoon. Around 11:00 p.m., when the married couple's house lights went out, the shivaree party circled the house, honking car horns, ringing cowbells, singing, and cheering. Well-wishers banged wooden spoons on pots and pans, crashed pan lids together, and whistled and yelled to wake the newlyweds. After everyone had made all the noise they could, the newlyweds came out and invited folks in for drinks or treats.

Vacations

The only vacations we took were to rural Manvel, North Dakota, to visit Mom's relatives. Our lives were shaped by the schedule of milking dairy cattle twice a day, so we did not take these trips until Warren was old enough to do the milking alone.

By the seventh day God had finished the work he had been doing;
so on the seventh day he rested from all his work.
–Genesis 2:2 (NIV)

CHAPTER 28

Community Culture

The nearly self-contained Dalton community in which I grew up consisted of families from the town as well as the surrounding farms. Town folks earned a living by serving the farming community, and the farm families relied on the services and businesses in town. Lifelong relationships were built upon trust, sharing, and caring. Most people in the area had parallel beliefs and exhibited similar behaviors. Elements of life such as religion, ethnicity, geography, and family practices were nearly identical for everyone in and around Dalton.

Our community appeared healthy because there was not a great disparity of income—no one was too rich and no one was too poor. Affluent people were considered to be those who lived in the big cities and signaled their wealth by driving a luxury car, wearing expensive clothing, and taking expensive vacations.

Pride of Heritage

The Dalton community comprised a tightly woven web of likeminded third- and fourth-generation immigrants from Norway who, for the most part, worked hard and sustained the values of honesty, charity, and love of family. Norwegian immigrants settled Dalton in the latter half of the nineteenth century. One of these was my great-grandfather, Berger Erickson. In 1852, at the age of twenty-seven, he came to America, making the voyage on a sailing vessel, which required more than nine weeks for the journey. He brought along his wife and one-year-old son, and they settled in Wisconsin. After serving in the Civil War and then farming in Wisconsin, he moved his family to Dalton in 1871. The entire family moved by ox team and covered wagons, across the woods and prairies to Otter Tail County, Minnesota, where they bought 120 acres of state land in section 36, Dane Prairie Township, north of Dalton. Berger and his wife had fourteen children. The oldest son received the farm, and in 1880 another son, Cornelius Erickson, bought land two miles south of Dalton, which is our home today. Cornelius passed the homestead on to his son Palmer (my grandfather) who in turn passed it on to Milton (my father). I tell this story because it is typical of so many of the homesteads and families in the Dalton community.

Most everyone in Dalton had relatives in close proximity. Our Norwegian-American community was proud of our heritage, and we expressed that through ethnic cuisine and social traditions. Until my Catholic mother came to town, everyone in Dalton was Lutheran. Most people attended church on Sunday and were active in Ladies Aid and the Luther League.

As a fourth-generation immigrant, Dad's first language was Norwegian, and he retained many Norwegian mannerisms. Everyone in the area shared a common speech pattern with a strong Norwegian accent. Grandma even wrote and received letters in Norwegian. Perhaps the greatest behavior similarity was the Norwegian sense of humor and ability to have a good time, along with a love for stories and exaggeration.

Shared Beliefs and Behaviors (Social Norms)

The 1950s was a decade marked by certain societal rules. Dalton had its own character, with its own specific weaknesses and strengths. Most of us shared the same values—we believed in doing what was right, being honest, sharing, and working hard. Perhaps our greatest disadvantage was our limited exposure to other cultures.

Dalton natives valued family, traditions, holidays, and respect for the elderly. Relatives lived in the same community, helping to make it strong and intact. When farmers and their wives retired, they would turn their farm over to a son and move to a small house in Dalton.

Farms remained in the same family for generations, and local businesses had little (if any) turnover. People identified with this place. Farm families cherished their land—it had a value much greater than economics. Our relationship to the land was best summed up by something Margaret Mitchell wrote in *Gone With the Wind:* "Land is the only thing in the world that amounts to anything, for 'tis the only thing in this world that lasts. 'Tis the only thing worth working for, worth fighting for . . ."

Very few women worked outside the home. Dad's role was a farmer and Mom's role was a homemaker. Dad rarely did common household chores; but he did help Mom paint, hang storm windows, and do other chores that required strength. Dad was in charge of things like car maintenance, remodeling, and fixing a broken screen door or a rusty hinge. I do not believe Dad ever changed a diaper, did the laundry, or made a bed. Likewise, Mom did very little farm work. She rarely went in the barn, never drove a tractor, and did not work with any of the animals except the chickens. However, Mom and Dad balanced the checkbook and prepared the taxes together.

Childcare usually fell to Mom and us older kids. As an older sibling, I read to the little kids, bathed them, monitored their catechism lessons, entertained them, put them to bed, and babysat when Mom was gone. Both Dad and Mom supervised us kids since we had both farm chores and household chores to perform. Our parents were actively involved in our education, social outings, and 4-H activities.

Families were remarkably stable. Marriages were valued and divorce was rare, so children were raised in two-parent homes. Pregnancies out of wedlock were considered mortifying, and usually the couple "had to get married." Parent, teachers, and elders were respected and obeyed.

I never heard Dad tell an off-color joke or cuss, and women did not swear or smoke. My parents' age group was the first generation in our family to drink socially. Grandma did not consider it acceptable, especially for women.

"Saving face" was important. Being indebted by borrowing or receiving favors made us uncomfortable. Bankruptcy and accepting charity were considered dishonorable.

Non-confrontation was the norm; and out of respect for others' opinions, we did not talk about religion or politics. In our Norwegian culture, it was not appropriate to be frank about emotions, about the reasons behind a conflict or a misunderstanding, or about personal information.

Feeling safe was a condition of our generation. We trusted almost everyone and were open to strangers. People did not steal, and we left our front door unlocked. For me, danger lurked in a herd of cows stampeding, thoughts of drowning in the pond or water tank, or falling through the ice.

Social Etiquette

Men always vacated a seat for a woman or someone elderly. "Please" and "thank you" were compulsory. Men never wore a hat indoors, and they took it off if they were talking to a woman. If you saw a lady struggling with her shopping, you would offer to help. Men always opened the door for women and allowed them to enter or exit first.

Patriotic Citizens

As with others in the community, the Bergerson men always stepped up to answer the call of duty and serve in the military. Berger Erickson arrived in the United States in 1852, and in 1864 and 1865 served in the Civil War with Company D, Eighteenth Regiment, Wisconsin Volunteer Infantry, taking part in several engagements while in the service. Grandpa Palmer served in World War I, while two of his sons served in World War II.

Town Kids and Farm Kids

I felt that the farm kids and town kids were equals. We attended the same school and dressed the same, so we were the same. I had friends in town; and, although I knew they did not carry the same workload as the farm kids, I never resented it. We had skating parties, birthday parties, and slumber parties. I knew my life would be like the town kids' lives once I graduated from college. I had no desire to be a farm wife.

There were many things farm kids had that town kids desired, such as 4-H activities and riding horses. In fact, some town kids even joined 4-H.

Artistic Expression and Organized Sports

Although academia was highly valued, the arts were not a high priority. We were not an artistic community in the sense of attending concerts, the theater, or art exhibitions. Music was what we heard on the radio, theatre consisted of the annual school Christmas play, and art exhibitions were the beautiful handiwork creations our grandmothers made.

It would have been hard to have any cultural influences from television because we did not have one. We did listen to a lot of music—from Mom's radio in the kitchen, Dad's radio in the barn, and records on the phonograph player. Everything we listened to was country western.

Our small-town life may not have afforded much cultural or artistic appreciation, but we were instilled with a drive for intellectual pursuits.

The Exodus

The exodus from the Dalton community started with my generation. Lured by higher education, better jobs, and distant opportunities, we left the countryside to find our fortunes under the glow of city lights. The small farms and villages began to vanish, giving way to cities and progress. School mergers further echoed the countryside's crisis. All of the siblings left except for Daryl. One went to Boston, one to San Francisco, one to St. Louis, and the rest to Minneapolis.

If it is possible, as far as it depends on you,
live at peace with everyone.
–Romans 12:18 (NIV)

CHAPTER 29

Our Town

Dalton was named after Ole C. Dahl, who donated land for railroad tracks and a depot, by which the growing town was anchored. White houses, some one-story and some two-story with well-kept lawns, flowers, and lots of trees, made up the town. Most of the businesses on Main Street were owned by the same families for several decades, so there was little turnover in the population.

Businesses on Main

Everyone in Dalton lived within walking distance of the businesses on Main Street, which was about a block long. Most of the stores were built close together and had large plate-glass windows for their storefronts. Shopkeepers knew your name, or at least what family you belonged to; and they greeted you with a smile. A tactful and gracious respect existed between business owners and customers, with both sides valuing the other. Business owners asked a fair price and allowed farmers to charge their purchases until the monthly milk check came in. In return, farmers remained loyal to local businesses, buying groceries, gas, jeans, and appliances only from people in town.

A post office, village hall, bank, hardware store, general store, grain elevator, lumberyard, grocery store, two cafés, two filling stations, a general merchandise store, the vestige of an old hotel, and two implement dealers lined Main Street. In addition, our town had two churches, a school, a hatchery, a grain elevator, a barbershop, and a creamery. We did not have a pharmacy, doctor, dentist, police officer, or library. We went to Fergus Falls if a doctor was absolutely necessary. A barbershop for men was located in the basement of the barber's house.

My great-uncle Hilmer owned a farm implement business where Dad purchased barbed wire, twine, wire, tools, and other farm equipment. When he was busy in the field, Dad dispatched one of us girls to ride our bike to the store and get a part for him. Sometimes it was necessary to go to town unexpectedly because a piece of broken farm equipment had to be replaced or repaired at the blacksmith's shop.

The hardware store sold hardware and appliances, household utensils, washing machines, toys, and gifts. At the filling station, the attendant washed our windshield, checked the oil and tires, and pumped the gas. The creamery sold milk and ice cream, had an egg operation, and maintained the locker plant. Dad went to the bank once a month to deposit his creamery check, and one of us usually went along.

The general store sold coffee, sugar, flour, spices, and other household staples. Denim work shirts, overalls, caps, mittens, work gloves, and men's Red Wing work shoes jammed the shelves.

This was also the place to buy fabric, thread, lace, ribbon, and sewing notions.

Penny Candy

"Secure your money in a hanky so you won't lose it," Mom cautioned us girls before we pedaled our bikes to Dalton to spend part of our allowance.

At the general store, standing in the alluring candy aisle for an indeterminate time, we contemplated what to purchase. For one cent, we could buy a Tootsie Roll, red wax lips, a black licorice pipe, Bazooka bubble gum wrapped in a comic strip, Topps baseball cards with a pink slab of hard bubble gum, lipstick candy in a one-inch tube with gold foil around it, or long straw Pixie Stix filled with candy powder. Five cents bought a pack of Blackjack gum, a necklace of candy beads, a six-pack of wax bottles filled with sweet syrup, or candy cigarettes. Five-cent candy bars included Baby Ruth, Butterfinger, Milky Way, Heath Bars, Bit-O-Honey, and Three Musketeers. I favored a Walnut Crush in a shiny orange wrapper with dark chocolate and a white nougat filling. The grocer trusted us and tolerated our dawdling as we scrutinized the penny candy selections. Once we'd made our decision, he put our candy in a small brown paper bag and thanked us for our purchase.

Running Errands

Farmers who hauled their milk and cream cans to town stopped to get meat at the locker plant, purchased a few items their wives wanted from the general store, and then stopped for coffee at one of the cafés. Before heading home, they picked up their mail from the mailbox in the post office. By afternoon, the main street was quiet.

Dad allowed one of us to tag along whenever he sold grain at the grain elevator, which was located along the railroad tracks. We waited in line until we could drive onto a scale before dumping our grain into a pit. The empty wagon was weighed again to figure the number of bushels Dad had delivered. Sometimes we would go to the office and wait. Dad dropped a dime in the pop machine and slid out a bottle of Hires Root Beer for me, and he put a penny in a different machine to get a handful of peanuts.

Entertainment

In the summer months, we went to town for Saturday Night Drawings, hosted by local business owners. Mom visited with friends while she and the little ones sat in one of twenty cars angled on Main Street, while Dad dropped in at the café to play pool, and we older kids roamed around with our friends. At 8:00 they announced over the loudspeaker who had won $25, $10, and $5 prizes redeemable at a local merchant.

Eating out was something our family never did. In fact, I did not know any family who ate out. When I was fourteen, I started working at a café in town. Most of our business came from the men who were building the new superhighway. I think cafés were more places to socialize over coffee than to actually eat a meal. People would become regulars at a café. One café stayed open until 9:00 or 10:00 p.m. High school kids gathered there to put nickels in the jukebox and sip Cokes.

The Big City

Before the interstate was built, a trip to Fergus Falls took a half hour, so we did not go often except for church. Our family, like most families, believed in shopping locally, but a couple times a year Mom drove Grandma and us girls to Fergus Falls to browse the McCall's and Simplicity pattern books. We strolled by the big city stores on our way to Woolworth's Five & Dime, where Grandma purchased thread, buttons, and rickrack. I first rode on an escalator and observed a money trolley at the S&L Store. Rather than count change, clerks put money in a canister that rode along a cable from the first-floor cash register to the upper-level balcony, where an employee accepted the payment and returned the correct change by way of the trolley.

Do not forget to show hospitality to strangers,
for by so doing some people have shown hospitality
to angels without knowing it.
–Hebrews 13:2 (NIV)

CHAPTER 30

4-H Country Club

In addition to school, the Dalton 4-H Club was our main social get-together, connecting us to new friends from other rural schools in Ottertail County. 4-H activities included family-orientated entertainment, meetings, picnics, parties, and hayrides; but most of all 4-H promoted a sense of belonging and inclusiveness among members. The parent leaders empowered the 4-H members and taught leadership skills as they allowed young people to have a role in decision making. We older members held offices, chaired committees, and conducted meetings.

Gathering at the Dalton school once a month, we elected officers, presented programs, and planned activities. We recited the 4-H creed, read secretary and treasurer reports, and voted to have the annual Halloween and Christmas parties. When the meeting adjourned, parents visited over coffee and bars while we kids wandered through the school to places teachers usually forbid us to explore.

One of our first fall social functions was a hayride. While a tractor pulled the hayrack stacked with square bales; we girls bunched together, laughing and giggling, as the boys roughhoused and threw hay at us. A bright harvest moon lit our way as we rode over winding dirt roads through the rural countryside. We sang songs and enjoyed a beautiful fall evening, the air cool and crisp, autumn smells filling the air. Returning to the farm, we sat around a crackling bonfire, mesmerized by dancing copper-colored flames and red-hot glowing embers while we roasted marshmallows on long sticks, drank hot apple cider, and enjoyed the camaraderie of wonderful friends.

October brought us the Halloween party, in December we had a bunco party, and in January we prepared for our annual Share-the-Fun Festival. At that event, some clubs performed choral numbers, instrumental pieces, or dance routines; our club performed a humorous theatrical skit. It gave us the opportunity to work on vocal projection, entrances and exits, focus, transition, and movement, as well as selecting costumes and props. We learned teamwork by collaborating on our performance, costuming, creativity, and staging, but most of all we developed new friendships while having fun.

Instead of a July meeting, we had 4-H Visiting Day. 4-H club members, parents, and county extension agents caravanned from farm to farm to observe project animals. We ended the day with a wiener roast and a softball game.

County Fair

The most highly anticipated event of 4-H was the annual county fair. Ribbons and premiums were awarded in many classes of competition, although my primary goal was to have fun with my friends. Warren, Audrey, and I showed pigs at the county fair in Fergus Falls, which required us to remain there so we could feed and water them. We showed black-and-white Hampshire pigs and white Yorkshires.

In the days leading up to the county fair, we trained our pigs for exhibition. We tried to teach the pigs to turn right when we tapped them on the left shoulder and turn left when we tapped them on the right shoulder. To have them walk straight ahead, we tapped them between the shoulder blades. Unfortunately, our pigs never were able to learn these signals.

On the day of judging, we washed and brushed the pigs, patted their bristled backs with talcum powder and baby oil, and tried to curl their tails. Attired in black slacks and a white shirt, and carrying a bamboo cane, I paraded my three-hundred-pound heavyweight barrow into the dusty show arena. My showmanship consisted of following my barrow around the show ring rather than parading him around it. Dad said to let the judges get a favorable look at our pigs, so we tried to slow them down in front of the judges' viewing area. County Agent Nick Wyrhens said our goal was to learn how to raise a quality pig and to assume responsibility.

Dad knew how to select a worthy animal from our private stock with appropriate muscling and leanness, and every year we were awarded blue ribbons for our pigs, which made Dad proud. When the judges quizzed me, I remembered the stock answers Dad had formulated for me.

"How much do you feed your pig a day?" asked a judge.

"I'm a believer in self-feeding, so I let him eat as much as he wants. This allows him to grow as fast as possible. And I make sure he has water."

"How much weight does your pig gain a day?"

"Well, I figure a little over two pounds a day."

"What was the hardest part of raising your pig?"

"I have to check several times a day that my pig has water in his trough due to the fact that he loves to tip it over to cool off. Pigs don't sweat, you know."

"What is your pig's name, Miss?"

"My dad doesn't let us name the pigs. He tells us to be kind to them, but to keep in mind they're not pets to become attached to because they're only around for nine months."

"Smart dad," a judge laughed.

Judging finished, we enjoyed three days of complete freedom to eat cotton candy and snow cones, play midway games, listen to carnival music, go on amusement rides, visit exhibit barns and concession stands, and attend the grandstand. We congregated with friends at the horse barn, wandered through cattle barns, explored the pig and sheep exhibition pens, and rambled through the 4-H building to see food and sewing exhibits. When we got hungry, we stopped by our 4-H booth for free pasteurized chocolate milk and purchased a barbeque for twenty-five cents.

Dad gave us money to spend; and for ten cents a ride, we rode the Tilt-A-Whirl, Bullet, Octopus, Ferris wheel, merry-go-round, roller coaster, and bumper cars. We frequented a funhouse, a walkthrough amusement trailer featuring a moving walkway, mirror mazes, trick stairways, and dark passages as well as tilted rooms. We watched older kids win stuffed animals at midway booths, and we tried our luck at ring-the bottle, ring toss, tip-the-bear, and cranes.

And let us consider how we may spur one another on
toward love and good deeds.
–Hebrews 10:24 (NIV)

Dad Presenting
Eighth Grade Diploma
to Maxine

CHAPTER 31

Rural School

The American Dream

Some of the most rewarding and positive experiences of my life came from attending a three-classroom country school for eight years. There was no kindergarten, so we attended first through eighth grade. Dad and Mom ingrained in us that we lived in a country of equality and opportunity, and that hard work and a good education would give us hope and options in life. There were no barriers to attending college. Because of the 1958 Federal Student Loan Program, every American citizen could attend college if they chose to do so. We took our education seriously and accepted that our futures would take us away from Dalton.

Country School

For the eight years I attended the Dalton school, my class consisted of the same five kids—three boys and two girls. "Diversity" was represented by two kids who lived in town and three who lived in the country. The lower-grade room included first, second, and third grades; fourth, fifth, and sixth grades comprised the intermediate room; and seventh and eighth grades were in the upper-grade room. I always had a brother or sister in my classroom.

The total population of our small rural school consisted of three teachers and approximately fifty kids. How we were afforded three such excellent teachers, I do not know. Those same three teachers were there the entire time I attended the school. By the end of our eight years, we were well prepared for further academic study as we joined a class of three hundred ninth-grade students in Fergus Falls.

The Dalton school was a model of cleanliness because of Henry, our part-time custodian. There was also a part-time cook on staff. I tended to dislike the school meals, perhaps not so much because of the quality of the cooking but because the food was different from what we ate at home. The menu often consisted of hot-dishes, stewed tomatoes, goulash, and spaghetti.

The Schoolhouse

As you walked through the door of our schoolhouse, you faced a wide set of wooden stairs, one going up and one going down. The entryway wall was lined with cubes for our winter overshoes and ice skates.

Three classrooms with high ceilings, walls of windows, hissing radiators, and creaking hardwood floors were on the second floor of the square two-story brick schoolhouse, which was built in

1938. Framed portraits of George Washington and Abraham Lincoln hung above the blackboards (they were green, but we called them blackboards), and maps, globes, and a dictionary graced each room. The desks and seats were one-piece with a lift-up top, under which we kept our books and pencil cases.

A wonderful, if limited, library of books, a janitor's closet, a small storage room with a mimeograph machine, a sick room with a door to the fire escape, and a water fountain were also located on the second floor, along with the boys' and girls' lavatories. Most of us farm children did not have bathrooms at home (we were still using outhouses), so this was a nice bonus for us.

Downstairs, a large auditorium/gymnasium with a built-in stage served as a gym, cafeteria, music room, and community center. A big upright piano stood next to the stage, and we set up folding chairs for the students. The teachers played the piano while we sang "Little Brown Church in the Vale," "Red River Valley," "When Johnny Comes Marching Home," and "Fifteen Miles on the Erie Canal."

A woodworking shop, kitchen, and never-used shower rooms were also downstairs. During seventh and eighth grade, all students took woodworking, which was taught by Henry the janitor. In seventh grade, we made a maple leaf shelf. Henry cut it out, and we sanded and varnished it. In eighth grade, we made a magazine rack end table. Once again, Henry cut it out, and we sanded it and stained it. It was not long before my folks had a shelf and end table in every room of our house.

School Grounds

The playground had a huge slide, teeter totters, swings, monkey bars, a merry-go-round, and plenty of open area to play tag, run races, or play softball. We girls jumped rope and played hopscotch on the big doublewide sidewalk in front of the school. Hopscotch involved drawing a chalk diagram including the numbers zero to ten. The object was to throw a small stone into each numbered box in succession and then to hop into all the other boxes except the one marked with the stone.

During afternoon recess, boys and girls played organized games together such as pump-pump pull away, prisoners' base, kickball, punch ball, or kitten ball. I was not very good at hitting with a bat, but I could run fast and was good at kicking and punching the ball, so I was never the last one picked for a team. When the weather did not allow us to go outside, we played drop the handkerchief, musical chairs, or dodge ball in the gymnasium; or we did square dancing. Sometimes we marched, walking in pairs to music, following the lead couple. The lower grades played red light, green light; duck, duck, gray duck; the farmer in the dell; and musical chairs.

In December, one of our dads banked a large area on the playground and flooded it to make an ice skating rink. Every kid in school owned a pair of ice skates. The boys wore black hockey skates, and we girls wore white figure skates with homemade bright yarn pompoms. We skated during the noon hour, using the warming house with benches and an oil-burning stove to put on our skates. We especially enjoyed playing crack the whip. When we did not skate, we went sledding, using large flat pieces of cardboard.

Compulsory Education

Although education was compulsory, farm kids sometimes had to stay home during the critical planting and harvesting seasons. Nothing was said because everyone understood that farm families needed extra help during these times. The teachers knew that parents valued education and would not keep their children home if it were not necessary. Warren missed several days for planting, while we girls missed school for rock picking.

We did not have lessons in physical education, music, or art. Rather, we played games, sang songs, and made crafts. Our standard subjects were reading, penmanship, arithmetic, grammar, health, and social studies, and we received new math, penmanship, spelling, and reading workbooks each year. Science and "how to write" were not emphasized.

School started at 9:00 a.m. and went until 4:00 p.m. For slow learners there were no special services. Discipline consisted of staying after school, although farm kids could not because they were needed for chores. Special events and activities included making floats for the town celebration in September, the Halloween party, the Christmas program and party, caroling, Parents Visiting Day, the Valentine's Day party, Raking Day, and the spring picnic.

Our main art supplies were crayons, construction paper, and glue. In September, we cut out red, yellow, and brown leaves to hang on the windows. October heralded orange construction-paper pumpkins with triangular noses and eyes and silly grins, along with witches, ghosts, and skeletons with movable arms and legs. For Thanksgiving, we drew turkeys, Pilgrims, and Indians. In December, we cut Christmas trees from green construction paper and added a yellow star at the top. We made snowmen in January, and February found us pasting a doily behind a red heart. Rabbits were too hard for me to draw, so in March I colored construction-paper Easter eggs. We made umbrellas for April showers and flowers for May.

The town fire siren rang at noon, signaling the time for town kids to walk home for lunch. President Harry S. Truman began the national school lunch program in 1946, so the Dalton school offered a hot lunch for farm kids. Meat was never served on

Friday—a caring gesture quite appreciated by my parents. We sang "Bless This House" before eating a hot lunch at school. The rule was that we had to sit at the table until we ate our food. We usually didn't like the food, so we became adept at stashing it in our milk cartons.

A county superintendent came out once or twice a year to see if our school was following the state and federal rules. He or she also brought the Iowa Test of Basic Skills, which we took each spring. My father was on the school board for all of the years I can remember.

Transportation

On warm fall and spring days, Warren and I pedaled our single-speed Huffy bicycles with coaster brakes one mile to school. Jo and Audrey rode on the handlebars or the back fenders. On the winding gravel road into Dalton, we cycled by a pasture and a slough, rode past farmer Eddie's place, and climbed the north hill. Before reaching Dalton, we crossed the railroad tracks; weaved through the businesses in Dalton, including the hatchery, Lutheran church, and post office; and turned right at the north end of town onto the street where Grandma lived and where the school was located. Sometimes if we arrived early we visited Grandma.

When temperatures dropped too much to ride bikes, or when it rained, we squeezed into Dad's pickup truck cab and rode along on his milk delivery to the creamery. Once we were piled in the truck we sang: *"I'm Moo Moo the cow/I eat lots of hay/I sit on the tracks/For most of the day/My milk is so good/It doesn't take long/For all little children/To grow big and strong."*

Primary Room

Every day of school was memorable. Mrs. Halvorson was my teacher for first, second, and third grade. On the first day of school, I ran up the wide wooden stairs with my red Big Chief wide-lined tablet, a red two-drawer pencil box, three pencils, a sixteen-count crayon box, and an eraser. The teacher gave me a desk, a colorful math workbook, a Palmer penmanship book, and a *Before We Read* book. These were the most treasured gifts I had ever received.

Each school day commenced with the Pledge of Allegiance and Show and Tell before Mrs. Halvorson called different grades to the table. We learned to read pictures before we read words, and we developed a relationship with Dick, Jane, Sally, Spot, and Puff. We learned to read left to right and to follow the teacher's oral directions as we colored pages in our first pre-reading workbook. I found it exhilarating having a readiness book to color in.

Next, we embarked on the first of three pre-primers, learning vocabulary in increased difficulty levels through sight-reading. We had an ambitious goal: to read like the adults. In the afternoons we ventured into *Through the Green Gate*, featuring Susan, Bill, and Perky the dog. Never did we read about a farm family, though once a year Susan and Bill visited their grandparent's farm.

Intermediate Room

In fourth grade, I entered the intermediate room. My teacher, soft-spoken and nurturing Miss Moen, was my favorite teacher of all time. Each child held a special place in Miss Moen's heart, and she made an effort to ensure that all kids were accepted.

Miss Moen, a single woman and a "paragon of virtue," remained private about her personal life. We knew little more than she resided with her sister in Fergus Falls and drove to Dalton for school. We assumed she preferred to lead a secluded, modest, and simple life and was satisfied with her life's mission of teaching children. A modest dresser, she wore a straight black skirt, black laced-up two-inch-high granny oxfords, a tailored blouse closed at the neck with a cameo brooch, and a sweater draped over her shoulders.

One cold winter day, as Dad dropped us off late, I draped my ice skates over my shoulders as I ran into school. One ice skate swung and broke a glass panel in the door. Warren ran to tell Miss Moen this exciting news. As I walked in the room, Miss Moen came to meet me, put her arms around my shoulder, and assured me she knew it was an accident; though she said I needed to tell my dad. Later that evening, Dad said, "I know it was unintentional. However, I will hold you accountable for this careless mistake." Dad made me pay for the windowpane.

Miss Moen trusted us to work in groups in the mimeograph room and the library. She let us escape outside to clean the felt erasers on the brick wall, allowed us to clean our paintbrushes in the custodian's room, and gave us permission to walk uptown for supplies. These privileges made us feel special.

Every year we strategized a theme for the Threshing Bee parade float. The year I was in sixth grade it was easy, since this was during the time when the first astronauts were selected, trained, and sent into space. The Soviet Sputnik, Project Apollo, rockets, and space programs permeated the *Weekly Reader*, so a space travel theme was an obvious choice. We used a cardboard refrigerator box from the hardware store to make a space ship. Our float would be a decorated hayrack pulled behind a tractor. We worked hard as a team on this project, and we felt proud of what we accomplished. Of course, we girls could not ride on the float because NASA's first seven astronauts were all men.

Upper-grade Room

My seventh- and eighth-grade teacher, Mrs. Rude, reminded me of Queen Elizabeth: classy, impeccably dressed, cultured, sophisticated, and reserved. We country kids considered her wealthy because she wore nice clothes, lived in a new house in town, and talked about visits to Minneapolis. She showed her pride as she talked about activities her children partook in, and she made it clear that anyone ambitious enough to go college could have this same lifestyle. I loved when she told me to prepare for college. She provided opportunities and treated us like high school students. Perhaps more than any other person, Mrs. Rude advanced the exodus of people from rural Dalton to urban America by telling us to "go out and amount to something." Mrs. Rude prepared us for life beyond Dalton.

In the spring of 1963, when I was in the seventh grade, Mrs. Rude took our classroom to the Cooper Theater in the Minneapolis suburb of St. Louis Park to see *How the West Was Won*. We also visited the observation deck atop the 447-foot Foshay Tower in downtown Minneapolis. Experiencing a panoramic movie in Cinerama was perhaps the most exciting cultural outing of my childhood. For weeks we talked about the 105-foot curved screen, the orange round building, orange seats, and black walls of the theater, as well as the drapes that dramatically opened to reveal the movie screen. The family saga in the film covered several decades of westward expansion in the nineteenth century, including the Gold Rush, the Civil War, and building railroads. All the way home we sang "Raise a Ruckus." "Home in the Meadow" and "Shenandoah" still remind me of our field trip to Minneapolis. Our favorite movie stars became Debbie Reynolds, Henry Fonda, and Gregory Peck.

Mrs. Rude checked out old science or health filmstrips from the county superintendent's office and on Friday afternoons we lowered the shades, turned off the lights, and watched in awe. In the spring, we raked the school grounds, and neighboring schools came for Field Day, which included relay races, kitten ball, broad jumps, and gunnysack races.

Mrs. Rude gave us unlimited time to study for the eighth-grade County Test since test performance reflected on the teacher as much as the kids. Notes went out to our parents advising that children should go to bed early the night before and eat a good breakfast the day of the test.

Our parents never helped us with homework—we just figured it out on our own. Dad believed that knowledge and memorization were two different things, and rote memorization was not the same as learning. Knowing that three times three equals nine does not do you any good unless you understand it. You either learned facts or you learned how to think. Grades were important, but behavior was more important.

Eighth-grade graduation was a milestone in our lives. Dad, the school board chair, handed out diplomas, and the top student delivered a speech. After the ceremony, we entertained friends and relatives at our house, serving rice salad, pressed chicken sandwiches on homemade buns, Chinese chew bars, pastel mints, mixed nuts, and coffee. The three teachers as well as school board members, friends, and relatives attended my party.

On the last day of school, I stood in the small library alone, holding back tears, knowing I must leave a place I loved. It was time to move on, to embark on a new life. I was becoming an adult, and it was time to break the secure bonds with my family and small community. The end of eighth grade brought big changes to my life, and change is hard if what you are leaving behind is something you love. Since I was a toddler, I had known I would go to high school in Fergus Falls and then away to college. I knew I wouldn't live in Dalton when I graduated—I would pursue life in the big city—but I didn't know it would hurt so much. I did not know what my future held; but I knew it was time to spread my wings, and somewhere within me, lying dormant, was a desire for adventure.

I started ninth grade by riding a bus to Fergus Falls for an hour each way, not knowing the three hundred kids in my class, and without a welcoming or introduction. This experience was one of the hardest adjustments I've experienced in my life.

How much better to get wisdom than gold,
to get insight rather than silver!
–Proverbs 16:16 (NIV)

PART EIGHT

Serious Subjects

On Our Way to Church

CHAPTER 32

Religious Influences

Religion was an isolated part of our lives. My siblings, my mom, and I were Catholic, and everyone else in our community was Lutheran. Catholic and Lutheran religious convictions remained exclusive during the 1950s. Prejudice against individual traditions, practices, and beliefs prevailed. Little effort was made to understand commonality on larger principles. Catholics and Protestants disagreed on many issues—the authority of the pope, the role of the sacraments, the place of tradition and Scripture. Each denomination's spiritual pride closed the door on unity.

This bias was evident when Massachusetts Senator John F. Kennedy ran for president in 1960. Our country had never had a Catholic president, and the question some raised regarding Kennedy was whether he could be a loyal American while being a Catholic.

John Kennedy addressed these concerns in a historic speech on September 12, 1960, by stating, "I believe in an America where religious intolerance will someday end—where all men and all churches are treated as equal—where every man has the same right to attend or not attend the church of his choice . . . where no religious body seeks to impose its will directly or indirectly upon the general populace . . . and where religious liberty is so indivisible that an act against one church is treated as an act against all." John F. Kennedy was elected president of the United States in 1960.

Mixed Marriage

Mom held a nonnegotiable adherence to Catholicism, even though she was the only Catholic in her new community. Her religious views derived from an unquestioning confidence that Catholic religious beliefs, rituals, traditions, and authority provided the sole salvation for her. Mom's well-intentioned religious loyalty was a tribute to her persistence of faith, yet she was in a spiritual prison when it came to obeying religious rules. She never considered that everyone else was wrong, as she bore her religious rules and burdens alone.

When my Lutheran dad and Catholic mom married in 1947, society labeled it a "mixed marriage." Mom's father did not allow his family to witness the ceremony because Mom elected to marry "outside her religion." I believe he wanted to attend for the daughter he loved, but the religious rules and dogma of his church had led him to believe he could not rejoice in his daughter's union. The Catholic Church permitted my parents to exchange vows in the parish rectory but prohibited a ceremony in the church sanctuary. So, with two witnesses in attendance, they married in the parish house, under the condition that Dad sign a paper agreeing to raise his children as Catholics. Today it is hard to understand such harsh judgments, but the times have changed greatly concerning religion.

Dad's Faith

Dad did not attend church, but he was a Christian seven days a week. He demonstrated his love of God by loving all people, not just family and friends. He was an ethical and caring person who chose love over hate, compassion over mistrust, understanding over justice, and honesty over hypocrisy. He believed that behavior was more important than traditions and rituals. For Dad, faith meant helping a neighbor; respecting, supporting, and being kind to all people; treating animals humanely; spending time with his mother; and loving and being faithful to his wife and family.

Vatican II

My formative religious years were prior to the reforms of Vatican Council II. To be a "good Catholic," it was vital to abide by the commandments and rules of the church. Mom dogmatically aspired to instill in us children the importance of attending Mass, going to confession, praying the rosary, and respecting the Holy Days of Obligation. But for me, it was about rules, not faith.

We trekked to Fergus Falls every Saturday for Catechism class and every Sunday to attend church services. At that time we considered the trip to Fergus Falls a far distance (it took about thirty minutes); so we only went there for church, Catechism, and occasional shopping trips.

Nothing took priority over attending church on Sundays and Holy Days. Adorned in our Sunday best, including hats and gloves, we attended Mass at 6:30 a.m. If we forgot our hat or mantilla, we attached a handkerchief to our head with bobby pins. Entering the church, we blessed ourselves with holy water; walked by the baptismal font, the huge stained-glass windows, and the red vigil candles burning under the statues; genuflected before entering our pew; prayed on the wooden kneelers; and then sat to observe the altar boys lighting candles.

Not understanding Latin liturgy, we followed the Mass in our own missals, which provided the prayers in Latin on the left-hand pages with English translations on the right. We stood for the entrance song and procession, remained standing for the Introductory Rites (Sign of the Cross and Greeting, the Act of Penitence, the Gloria, and the Collect), sat for the Liturgy of the Word, stood for the "Alleluia," sat to listen to the homily, stood for the profession of faith, sat as the altar was prepared for the Liturgy of the Eucharist, watched the ushers pass offertory baskets, *remained* kneeling until it was time to go forward and receive Holy Communion, walked to the altar, knelt at the rail for communion, and returned to our pew and knelt for prayerful meditation. We stood for the blessing and dismissal, and then we exited and ran for the car, with each kid attempting to be first to get a window.

The season of Lent was the most difficult part of being Catholic in a Lutheran community. Following the 1950s rules and compliances of the Catholic Church, we fasted and abstained from eating meat on Friday, said the rosary every evening while kneeling on the hard linoleum dining room floor, and gave up candy for Lent.

Saturday Catechism classes were not a positive experience. Nuns monitored our lessons as we moved through the Baltimore Catechism. Although we memorized and recited, we did not discuss or understand. It was about rules, not faith. We walked in, took a chair, and recited our memorized verses without socializing or having fun with fellow attendees. We received Holy cards, scapulars, and metals of saints for our efforts. They taught us that the Catholic Church was the "one true church."

At the end of each Catechism class, we were directed to the tiny, dark confessional booth in the church, where we knelt and whispered through a screen to a priest.

"Bless me, Father, for I have sinned," I would say.

"How long has it been since your last confession?"

"One week," I answered.

"What are your sins?" the priest asked.

"I told two little white lies and was mean to my brother."

"Say two Hail Marys and one Our Father."

I never had to admit to the mortal sin of eating meat on Friday or missing Sunday Mass, because Mom would not allow us to commit those sins. Instead I used the generic sins of "I was mean to my brother or sister," "I talked back to my parents," or "I told a little white lie." These, of course, were venial sins, so I would not have to burn forever in the fires of hell.

In the 1960s, there were enormous changes in the Catholic Church because of the reforms of the Second Vatican Council, but this was after my childhood. Unfortunately, I grew up with "head knowledge" of Jesus but no "heart knowledge." I never met the God of love as a child.

Missing a Family Bible

We did not have a Bible in our house, even though we were Christians. At that time, our Catholic church emphasized the Baltimore Catechism and not the Bible. Erroneously, Mom did not believe her religion wanted her to read the Bible—in fact, she believed the Bible was a Protestant thing. It was years later that I realized the Bible is the Christian message and endorsed by all Christian religions, whether Catholic or Protestant.

When it came to Bible knowledge, most of what I learned was from the Christmas carols we sang in school that focused on the celebration of Jesus' birth. "Away in a Manger," "O Little Town of Bethlehem," "Silent Night," "O Holy Night," "We Three Kings," "Hark! The Herald Angels Sing," "Angels We Have Heard on High," "The First Noel," "Go Tell It On the Mountain," "Joy to the World," and other carols that we sang every day in public school were the foundation of my biblical education. Actually, most of these songs were traditional rather than biblical, but they at least exposed me to bits and pieces of what was in the Bible.

Faith Lives in Community

Throughout my childhood, our community life was centered on school, the church, and 4-H. I remember feeling deprived that I could not go to the same church as my grandma and all of my friends. Only later was I able to understand that it was not Catholicism I was rejecting; it was the separateness, not being able to do what other kids did, not being one of them. I always felt accepted except when it came to religion. Distance and time were the roadblocks preventing us from interacting and being part of our "out of town" church in Fergus Falls. We did not have the privilege of being known or of experiencing oneness and harmony with our fellow members. We were not in church for the fellowship. After the service, we went home to do chores rather than staying to commune with the other parishioners.

Although there was no religious intolerance from the community, I must admit I felt uncomfortable being different from our friends. Group identities were important to me as a kid, and I wanted to belong. To be different in one area of your life when you are a child is not fun.

One of the strongest associations for Norwegian people in Dalton was the Lutheran church, a place for fellowship as well as worship. Perhaps because my dad, Grandma, and relatives all belonged to the Lutheran church in Dalton, we were still able to enjoy some of its comfort and warmth.

When Lutheran friends asked us to attend their Luther League events such as roller-skating and summer camps, Mom graciously approved. In fact, Mom attended most Ladies Aid events with Grandma Galena. We went with Grandma to mother-daughter banquets, and we attended all of our relatives' weddings, showers, and funerals at the Lutheran church. Mom worked in the kitchen, helping serve for these functions; and it is no surprise that when we girls got married, the Lutheran church hosted our community bridal showers.

Disconnected Credence

There was a disconnect with religion that made me uneasy. At that point in history, the Catholic Church taught that their church was infallible. This was disturbing, because I was not able to handle the idea that Dad, Grandma, and my friends were not going to heaven because they were Lutheran. They prayed. They loved God. They were people of principle and integrity. Their lives were guided by religious beliefs. Grandma and Dad had an unequaled compassion and respect for people. The hypocrisy I felt every time I thought about this was exacerbated by the fact that we did not talk about our Christian beliefs.

We were never devalued because of our religion, perhaps because of Dad's place in the community; but our arrangement made it hard to acquire a religious identity in childhood. For us, religion was a matter of attending church with no connection to the Catholic community. We felt like we did not belong.

Mom and Dad handled complex religious issues by ignoring them, leading to unacknowledged confusion and disconnected credence for us kids. I grew up in a religious atmosphere of great tolerance but little questioning. Communication, so valued and encouraged in our family, was stifled concerning doctrinal divides.

The lessons I learned during my childhood on the farm still influence me today. I was fortunate to have received a spiritual heritage from my mother, and I am glad she believed it was her job to instill spiritual values in us. As for me, I refused to believe that one denomination was correct.

[Let us] not give up meeting together,
as some are in the habit of doing,
but encouraging one another—
and all the more as you see the Day approaching.
–Hebrews 10:25 (NIV)

CHAPTER 33

Endless Conversation

A constant stream of discourse flowed through our family, whether we were eating, working, or playing. Many of those conversations are as clear to me now as if they'd happened yesterday. We talked about important topics while sharing family meals, and we enjoyed making each other laugh. I thrived on those discussions.

"What did you learn in school today?"
Everyone in the family sat together for meals, and no matter how much we enjoyed the food, we enjoyed the conversation even more. We were loud, we interrupted, we listened, we argued, we talked fast, and sometimes we laughed so hard that tears rolled down our cheeks. Many of our table conversations are indelibly stamped in my memory. They usually started with Dad asking, "What did you learn in school today?" We reported on the books

our teachers were reading to us and the books we were reading ourselves. We shared scores we'd received on spelling, math, and social
studies tests. We discussed who was absent from school, who got in
trouble, and funny things that had happened.

Space Exploration

The *Weekly Reader* and the *Fergus Falls Daily Journal* provided numerous topics of conversation. Space exploration was one
of the most fascinating things we discussed—it was just beginning,
and we were awed. In 1957 the Russians launched a satellite named
Sputnik 1. On May 5, 1961 Alan Shepard became the first American in space as the Freedom 7 spacecraft left the earth's atmosphere.
In 1962, astronaut John Glenn was the first American to orbit the
earth; he went around three times and returned successfully.

John F. Kennedy

During the 1960 presidential campaign, John F. Kennedy
was trying to prove that a Roman Catholic could be president. We
did not want to ask in school why people were scared to have a
Catholic president, so we asked Dad. "Doesn't make sense to me,"
Dad said. "I'm voting for him." Of course Dad always voted for the
Democratic candidate.

Cold War, Communism, and the Cuban Missile Crisis

We often discussed the Cold War and Communism. I remember feeling scared that we would be bombed when the Russian missiles were delivered to Cuba during the 1961 Bay of Pigs
crisis. We told our parents that President John F. Kennedy wanted

us to build a bomb shelter in our basement and keep it stocked with food. "Well, I reckon you kids don't need to worry about that," was Dad's firm answer.

During the Cuban Missile Crisis, we were all afraid that Cuba would launch nuclear missiles toward the United States; and we would die a horrible death. When all was said and done, we as a country were extremely proud of how our young president, John F. Kennedy, had handled the situation.

Two New States

When Alaska and Hawaii became states in 1959, someone asked Mom if she knew we had two new states. "Well, of course. I wasn't born yesterday," Mom said.

"Do you think we will ever visit them?" someone asked.

"Quite unlikely," said Dad. "Mom and I have only visited North Dakota."

Racial Segregation

The *Fergus Falls Daily Journal* covered all the latest news, including conflicts over equality and inclusion for blacks. Confusion fell like a heavy blanket over the table when we discussed the racial segregation that was prevalent in our country. Legally segregated school systems existed until 1954. We had never seen a black person, but we could not understand why they could not ride on the same buses as whites. "Doesn't make sense to me," said Dad. "We're all people. We all fought in the war together."

A Super Highway Across the Farm

In addition to broader topics, we also exchanged views on things closer to home, like the day Dad learned that President Eisenhower's new highway would be built across our farm. It was always called a superhighway and not an interstate highway.

"It's hard to imagine," said Dad. "They say there will be two lanes in each direction and cars will go fast on it." The highway would be a part of the great trunk highway system to be built throughout the United States—a big, broad national highway, crossing the nation from east to west and eliminating all possible curves.

Bantering, Teasing, and Joking

Humor was our family's love language. We jested with those we cared for; it was our way of saying, "I like you." We learned to laugh at ourselves by telling a story expressively and enthusiastically, often by exaggerating. We enjoyed making other family members laugh, and we often busted out in hysterical laughter. Everyone tried to top one another with an outlandish story. Dad's humor, the way he saw things, the way he thought, was spontaneous. Some of the conversations were so funny, I feel they must be chronicled.

"Do you want to know what I learned in school today?" asked Daryl. Before anyone could answer, he jumped out of his chair. "We learned to Hokey Pokey like this," he sang as he danced. "You put your left foot in, you put your right hand in . . . "

"Daryl, for goodness sake, sit down. We are eating. You can show us later," said Mom.

Roars of laughter filled the room.

"Were you a star at the Hokey Pokey?" Dad asked, wiping the tears from his eyes.

"Oh, for sure. I was the best. Everyone said so."

This is the day the LORD has made;
let us rejoice and be glad in it.
–Psalm 118:24 (NIV)

CHAPTER 33

Epilogue

The difficult thing about childhood is that you can never go back. Things change—attitudes, social landscapes, culture, and lifestyles. History is strewn with memories of things that no longer exist. Today there are few dairy farms in the community where I grew up; the cooperative creamery is gone, and my school is now an apartment complex.

Yet, recalling the past is important because we are the sum of all the events in our lives. The only way we can understand who we are and how we got to be that way is by studying what we've done and where we've been. Similarly, reviewing my own history helps me understand other people better, and it helps me understand change.

Family Life

Family meant unconditional love and acceptance. We did not earn or achieve our significance; rather, we felt valued and had a sense of belonging, free of conditions and unrestricted by our failings. Though my parents did not parade their affection, we came to understand love demonstrated through their personal sacrifices, trust, pride, shared time, fairness, and advocacy.

We acquired a great thirst for knowledge. My parents' greatest desire was to give us educational opportunities beyond theirs. When Warren announced, at age seven, that he was going to college, the rest of us followed his lead, spurred on by our parents. Seven siblings earned college degrees, diverged geographically when jobs and marriages took us to larger cities, and never returned to live in our rural area. Warren and Dave received National Merit Scholarships and chose careers in actuarial science. Audrey, Jo, Eydie, and Diane entered the business world, while I choose a career in education. Daryl owns and lives on the family homestead today.

Life was about kinship with the local community. As his father had done, Dad was engaged in civic responsibilities, serving on the school board and on the Tumili Township Board. Mom and Dad were involved in numerous social groups and bowling leagues. We were fortunate in that we were not geographically isolated, being only one mile from town. 4-H, school activities, friends, and relatives provided us with social opportunities and community involvement.

I took away a deep appreciation of my Norwegian cultural heritage. Although Mom maintained an Irish birthright, we kids were especially proud to be Norwegian because we flourished in a Norwegian community, shared life with Norwegian relatives and neighbors, became acclimated to Norwegian food, and celebrated Norwegian customs. We lived our entire childhoods with my father's relatives. As a family, most of the eight of us children remain close, spending considerable time together. We remain proud of our Norwegian heritage and roots.

Broadening Horizons

I realized I was naïve about many things when I started ninth grade in the big city of Fergus Falls. At home, radio was our medium—we did not own a television. Our parents only played country western music, so of course that was all I knew; we never listened to classical or popular music. We girls knew how to feed the cows, but we did not learn new dances by watching *American Bandstand*. We knew how to pick rocks, but we never had time to play a musical instrument in a band. We knew how to ride the swing rope in the haymow, but we never wandered through clothing stores to admire new styles. We spent more time babysitting than we ever did playing with friends.

My first "aha" moment came during my first week in college. I had rarely lived a day when I did not have to clean or cook, do chores, and help take care of the little ones. At college I lived in the dorm, and my meals were made for me. All I did was study and make my bed. I liked this lifestyle, but I was lonesome for family. My roommate, an only child raised in the city, complained about having to share the dorm bathroom with others. To me, it was more luxury than I had ever had.

Stop and Smell the Roses

If I heard it once, I heard it a hundred times from Dad: "Stop and smell the roses." He was telling us kids to enjoy the present and not worry about what will happen tomorrow. He told us that if a farmer continually worried about what the weather would do to his crops, he would have a miserable life. Dad believed we had to control our thoughts because we could not control how fast the crops grew, when spring would arrive, or if a newborn calf would be male or female. He knew that everything in nature and in farming had its natural time and tempo that humans could not control.

Perhaps it was becoming parents ourselves that made us realize Mom and Dad had done the best they knew how. They made sacrifices for us kids that they never resented. They sent us to college. They carried a burden of feeling that they had done an injustice to us by requiring us to work as much as we did.

The Family Farm

The land in the Bergerson name since 1880 belonged to Mom alone from 1983 (Dad's death) until her death in 2010. For twenty-seven years she lived frugally so she could retain ownership of the farm, present it to the next generation, and keep it in the family. This land meant a lot to her. This farm was her story. She lived on it with Dad for forty years; she raised her eight children there, and she kept the house working and thriving for four decades. Together, Mom and Dad worked hard and struggled to keep the land and improve the farm. I believe she felt it belonged to something bigger than herself. It had been in the family almost a century and a half.

Daryl bought the original farmhouse and farm buildings along with forty surrounding acres. Mom continued to rent out the farmland, which gave her enough money to live on when added to her Social Security. She could have sold the farm and indulged herself, but instead she chose to retain the land.

Mom and Dad left the entire farm, mortgage free, to their eight children, under the condition that we keep it in the family and not sell it. The decision of what to do with the land rested with

Mom. Owning land was an important enough reason for many of our ancestors to leave Europe and come to America. Mom and Dad, as well as each generation before them, built the farm through toil and perseverance.

Mom knew the land meant something to us kids—it was a part of us. We had explored every bit of the farm. We watched the crops mature and helped with the harvesting. This farm was the childhood playground we roamed. We knew the land, and we understood it.

What Mom did not realize is that the farm will not have the same meaning to her grandchildren, the children born to the eight of us. They never lived on the land. They never knew the inner workings of the farm. They never loved the land the way we did or felt that their lives were deeply intertwined with it. Deciding what to do with the family farm is a daunting task. My generation is at a point where no one can earn a living farming—or wants to. Small farms like this cannot provide for a family anymore. An era may end for the farm that has been in my family since 1885.

Alexandra Bergson, the proud steadfast character in Willa Cather's *O Pioneers!* summed it up this way: "We come and go, but the land will always be here. Those people who love and understand it are the only ones who really own it for a little while."

"For I know the plans I have for you," declares the LORD,
"plans to prosper you and not to harm you, plans to give you hope and
a future." –Jeremiah 29:11 (NIV)

PART NINE

Appendix

GRANDMA GALENA'S
RECIPE BOX

Chokecherry Juice

Chokecherry Jelly

Egg Coffee

Fattigmand

Julekake

Krumkake

Lefse

Lutefisk

Pickled Pig's Feet

Pressed Chicken

Pulsa (Pølse)

Rhubarb Pie

Rømmegrøt (Cream Porridge)

Rosettes

Rullepolse

Sandbakkels

Sotsuppe (Sweet Soup)

Spritz

Chokecherry Juice

1. Stem and wash chokecherries.
2. Cover with water in large kettle and bring to a boil.
3. Reduce heat and simmer one hour.
4. Drain through colander.
5. Then drain the juice though cotton dishtowel.
6. Pour into jars and seal for later making jelly or syrup.

Chokecherry Jelly

3 cups chokecherry juice
5 cups sugar
1 box fruit pectin

1. Boil chokecherry juice, sugar, and fruit pectin for three minutes.
2. Pour the hot jelly into hot sterilized glass jars to within one-
   quarter inch of the top. Pour a thin layer of paraffin over the
   top and let set. When the first layer has set, pour on a second
   layer of paraffin.

Egg Coffee

There was always coffee brewing in the kitchen, but for special occasions, we made egg coffee. Coffee made with an egg had a rich flavor. Grandma poured the coffee through a strainer as she poured it into a cup. Coffee was served with cream and sugar cubes.

1. Bring water to a boil in large white enamel coffee pot.
2. Add one cup of coffee grounds mixed with an egg to the boiling water.
3. Boil until the foam disappears.
4. Add 2 cups cold water to settle grounds to bottom.
5. Let it steep ten minutes before serving
6. The egg clings to the grounds, so when poured through a strainer, the result was a perfectly clear cup of coffee.

Fattigmand
(Fattigmand is a deep-fried diamond shaped cookie.)

6 egg yolks
1/3 cup sugar
1/2 cup cream, whipped
cardamom
2 cups flour

1. Beat eggs and sugar.
2. Add whipped cream, cardamom, and flour.
3. Place in refrigerator overnight.
4. Roll into thin sheets, cut in diamond shapes, and fry in lard.
5. Sprinkle with sugar.

Krumkake

(*Krumkake is* a wafer-like cookie baked in a special iron
and rolled into a cylindrical shape while still warm.)

1/2 cup butter

1 cup sugar

2 eggs

1 cup milk

1½ cups flour

1 teaspoon vanilla extract

1. In a bowl, cream the butter and sugar.
2. Add the eggs and mix using a wooden spoon.
3. Add the milk, flour, and vanilla, and mix well.
4. Heat the krumkake iron on medium heat on a stove burner, then put a teaspoon of batter on the bottom iron and press the top and bottom irons together. When brown on one side, turn and brown the other side. Remove from the iron and roll around a cone-shaped piece of wood while still warm.

Lefse

5 pounds white potatoes
½ cup butter
1 cup cream

1. First mash the potatoes with the butter and cream and next, rice the potatoes.
2. Mix together 2 cups riced potatoes, 1 cup flour, and 1 tablespoon sugar. Roll this mixture into small balls.
3. Roll the small balls flat to about 24 inches in diameter using three different rolling pins. Then roll it up on a lefse stick.
4. Bake on cast-iron stovetop or lefse griddle. Turn when it starts to bubble and turn brown.

Lutefisk

(Lutefisk is dried cod soaked in a lye solution. Every Christmas,
Dad purchased lutefisk from the general store in Dalton. Mom
served lutefisk for Dad and Grandma, every Christmas Eve.)

1. Rinse the lutefisk well, and place in a clean dishtowel or cheesecloth.
2. Boil in salted water for 5 minutes.
3. Remove from dishtowel and place on serving platter.
4. Serve with a pitcher of melted butter.

Pickled Pig's Feet

4 pig's feet (split in half)
3 cups cider vinegar
1 onion (sliced)
1 teaspoon pepper
3 whole cloves
1 bay leaf

1. Boil three parts vinegar and 2 part water, pepper, and spices. Pour over pig's feet.
2. Bring to a boil and skim off the foam.
3. Cook over medium heat until thoroughly done (approximately 2½ hours).
4. Store in a container with the liquid. Refrigerate. Serve cold.

Pressed Chicken

1 stewing hen

celery

onion

salt

pepper

1. Stew hen with celery, onion, salt, pepper, and water until chicken is tender.
2. Drain and reserve broth.
3. Discard skin, onion, and celery.
4. Remove meat from bones.
5. Chop meat with a knife and pack into a bowl.
6. Pour reserved broth over cut up chicken.
7. Press with plate in refrigerator.
8. Use for sandwich filling.

Pulsa (Pølse)

2½ pounds beef
2½ pounds pork
5 teaspoons salt
1 teaspoon pepper
½ teaspoon allspice
½ teaspoon ginger
1 medium onion
3 cups milk

1. Grind the pork and beef to the consistency of hamburger.
2. Add the seasonings and liquid, and put this mixture into washed pig casings.
3. When you are ready to prepare this sausage, prick the casing with a large needle, and boil for one hour.

Rhubarb Pie

3 cups fresh rhubarb, cut

1½–2 cups sugar

3 tablespoons flour

½ teaspoon nutmeg

2 eggs, well beaten

1 tablespoon butter

1. Pile rhubarb over lower crust.
2. Beat remaining ingredients and pour over rhubarb.
3. Add top crust and bake.

Rømmegrøt
(Porridge made of flour, butter, sugar, and cream)

1 quart cream

1 teaspoon salt

1¼ cups flour

3 cups milk

1. Boil cream for 20 minutes.
2. Stir in salt and flour.
3. Cook on low until butterfat comes to the top. Remove this butter.
4. Pour in boiling milk and stir.
5. When ready to serve, add the butterfat.
6. Serve warm with sugar and cinnamon.

Rosettes

Golden brown, crispy rosettes were one of our favorite holiday treats. They were made by dipping a metal iron (shaped like a star or a snowflake) into batter and then in hot grease.

2 eggs
1 tablespoon sugar
1/2 teaspoon salt
1 cup milk
1 cup flour

1. Beat eggs, sugar, and salt in mixing bowl.
2. Add milk and flour, and beat until smooth.
3. Melt lard in a deep saucepan.
4. Heat the rosette iron in hot lard and wipe excess oil from iron.
5. Dip iron into batter, but do not allow it to come over top of iron.
6. Put iron in hot oil. Fry for about 20 seconds or until desired color.
7. Shake rosette off iron.
8. When cool, dust with sugar.

Rullepolse

one shoulder of beef

onion

salt

pepper

1. Flatten on a board one shoulder of beef.
2. Cover with one diced onion, salt, and pepper.
3. Roll tight and tie with string.
4. Put in large pot and cover with water.
5. Simmer slowly for 3 hours.
6. Remove and place between plates under a heavy weight to press out moisture, until the roll is cold.
7. Remove string and slice thin for sandwiches. Serve cold.

Sandbakkels

(Sandbakkels are a cookie made of butter and flour,
baked in small fluted baking tins.)

1 cup butter

1 cup sugar

1 egg

1 teaspoon almond extract or cardamom

2 cups flour

1. Mix all ingredients together.
2. Press dough evenly and as thin as possible into fluted sandbak-
   kel molds.
3. Bake at 350° for 10 minutes.

Sotsuppe (Sweet Soup)

2 cups prunes

1½ cups raisins

1 cup apples

1 orange

2½ cups water

1¼ cups sugar

2 teaspoons lemon juice

1/3 cup tapioca

½ teaspoon cinnamon

1. Simmer prunes, raisins, apples, orange, and water for 1 hour.
2. Add sugar, lemon juice, tapioca, and cinnamon and stir until thick.

Spritz

1½ cups butter

2¼ cups sugar

2 eggs

1½ teaspoon vanilla

3½ cups flour

1. Cream butter and sugar.
2. Mix in beaten eggs, vanilla, and flour.
3. Pack into spritz cookie press and press onto cookie sheet.
4. Bake for 10 minutes.

990   Werner, Maxine Bergerson

Country Ragamuffins

DATE DUE
